A Checkerboard of Nights and Days

A Checkerboard of Nights and Days

A Memoir of My Cultural Journey

To Barbara
my best regard
[signature] Iran Fahmy

IRANDUKHT VAHIDI FAHMY

ISBN: 1983786802
ISBN 13: 9781983786808

I dedicate this book to my husband Mahmoud,
and to my three children,
Roya, Raef, and Randa

Tis all a Chequer-board of Nights and Days
Where Destiny with Men for Pieces plays
Hither and thither moves, and mates, and slays,
And one by one back in the Closet lays.

OMAR KHAYYÁM

Prologue

My family and friends huddled around me, handing me presents of Iranian sweets, nuts, and rice for my journey, pulling me into their arms for a last long hug, a final kiss.

"It's very cold in America," my aunt cautioned. "Make sure to wear your coat and scarf!" She handed me a beautiful red and cream-colored Persian blanket to take with me. "Do you remember how your grandfather always told you how vast and expansive the U.S.A. is? Make sure you don't get lost!"

My mother was crying as she told me how proud she was of me. "We'll see you again soon," she said through the tears. "You'll be back in Iran in just a few years."

I hardly heard what they were saying. In a few moments, I would be boarding a plane for the United States of America as a college student who had won a royal scholarship to attend any university of my choice in a new and strange land, leaving behind the only country and culture I had ever known.

Irandukht Vahidi Fahmy

Several months earlier, in August 1956, my mother, brother, and I had been visiting my favorite uncle, who lived in a large and spacious house in Rezaiyeh, my childhood city in the province of Azerbaijan in northwest Iran. His two-acre courtyard was surrounded by a six-foot tall wall; inside were breathtaking gardens, with flowerbeds full of roses, tulips, irises, pansies, and sunflowers, and a profusion of fruit trees—cherry, plum, pear, peach, and apricot. Late in the afternoon it was tea time—a staple of Iranian life. In the middle of his garden, a low, wooden table, sixteen-feet square, was placed among the trees and flowers and a colorful cloth (a sofreh) was spread upon it. A teapot brewed over a charcoal-heated samovar. The sofreh was laden with biscuits, cookies, sugar cubes, rose and cherry jam, a bowl of fresh fruit from my uncle's garden, cucumbers, white farmer's cheese, thin bread, and a basketful of herbs—parsley, green onion, leek, and coriander. We sat around the low table with our legs crossed on a colorful kilim (an outdoor rug) handmade by natives in the villages.

We drank the tea from small glasses while sucking on cubes of sugar, an Iranian custom. The cube melted upon impact with the warmth of the tea, providing a delicious burst of sweetness. As we chatted and gossiped with my uncle, his wife Attia Khanum, and their two young children Bejan and Faeza, I enjoyed the lovely garden scenery, and especially the luscious red and white grapes hanging from vines. They reminded me of my childhood, when I went to my maternal grandfather's winery to pick grapes.

Late in the afternoon my uncle approached us from the house. "Iran!" he called to me in excitement. "You need to go to Tehran as soon as possible!"

A Checkerboard of Nights and Days

"Why?"

He held the national newspaper *Ettela'at* and handed it to me.

"Here, read this! You won a special scholarship! You need to go to Tehran immediately!"

I glanced at the headline and read it aloud: *Twenty University Graduate Students Receive Royal Scholarships from the Shah to Study Abroad.* The article stated: "His Majesty the King, who has always been enriching and furthering the education of the younger generation, is offering a full scholarship to twenty top graduates of colleges and universities from different disciplines to study abroad."

My name was listed among the scholarship winners. We were to report to the Ministry of Education in Tehran by the first week in September.

My first reaction was doubt. "I wasn't informed of this!" I cried. "I didn't get any letters from the university!"

I thought it was nothing more than a publicity stunt, knowing the bureaucracy and inefficiency of the Iranian government. My mother, however, had no doubts as she jumped to her feet with excitement.

"Of course it's true. You graduated with honors. We must leave right now to prepare for your trip!"

In a calm voice, I told her we would leave the next day, and we did. My mother and I travelled by boat across Lake Rezaiyeh to

Tabriz, the largest city in the province of Azerbaijan and where I had lived for five years while I attended the university there. Two days later I took a ten-hour overnight bus ride to Tehran by myself, an arduous trip that crossed the Azerbaijan Mountains on very narrow roads. The next morning my brother Manoochehr, a third-year engineering student at the University of Tehran, picked me up at the bus stop and took me by taxi to my grandfather's house in the northern section of the city. My aunt opened the door, greeted me, and escorted me to my grandfather's room. He was sitting in his room on a comfortable chair with bookshelves surrounding him, wearing a white shirt, black pants, and a small hat. He greeted me with only a nod of his head. After a day of rest, I went to the ministry of education and met several of the other scholarship recipients. Ushered into the office of the study abroad program, I was informed that my assigned country was Switzerland, where I would study for my Master's and Doctorate in Education.

When I discussed this with my family, my sister Pooran, a high school English teacher, asked me, "Why Switzerland and not the United States? You do not speak French or German." A few days later I went back to the office and spoke with the government representative concerning my assignment.

"Is there any way I could go to the United States instead of Switzerland?"

He said "Swiss universities are best known for their programs in psychology and pedagogy. Also, tuition fees are much less in Europe than the United States."

A Checkerboard of Nights and Days

"But I've received a scholarship," I told him. "Shouldn't I have a choice in where I want to study?" He responded, "I will discuss it with my superiors."

A few weeks later I got a call from the office, informing me that I could go to a language institute in the U.S. to improve my English and receive an orientation to American culture. Then I would be free to attend any university of my choice in the U.S. My choice was Teachers College of Columbia University in New York City.

Weeks went by. There was no news about my departure for the rest of September and most of October. My initial doubts seemed to be confirmed. There would be no scholarship. The government was too incompetent to implement such a program. Then, one day in the middle of October, a representative from the ministry called to inform me that they were still awaiting confirmation of my admission from the U.S. In the meantime, I was assigned to teach math in a girls public high school in Tehran for two months.

Finally, in the third week of December, the twenty of us—four women and sixteen men—were invited to the Shah's palace to officially received our scholarships and thank His Majesty for his generosity. Now I had no doubt that I was finally on my way to the U.S. My dream had come true—I always knew that America was a land of opportunity, and now I looked forward to a new life, with the kind of freedom I had always longed for.

As I waited for the announcement to board the plane, I felt so divided—relieved and excited to be departing Iran, but also deeply sad about leaving my loved ones behind and anxious about adjusting to an entirely new country and culture. Although I cherished and respected many things about my country, I had always felt like a stranger in my native land. As a member of a minority religion, the Baha'i faith, the extremist Muslim majority considered us agnostics, not a God fearing or God loving people. As a woman, I felt isolated socially and emotionally. Although both genders were respected and treated as equals in my family, I felt restricted in a society that was male-dominated, where the sons of families were privileged, respected, and valued more than daughters. My family had long been westernized and none of the women in my family wore a hijab or abaya. And yet when I walked the streets of Tabriz without a scarf or a covering, men would stare at me harshly or even jostle against me to assert their authority, to show that they disapproved of my freedom. Some fundamentalist Muslims would not even make eye contact with me when they passed in the street. When I attended Tabriz University, ninety percent of the students were male and only ten percent were women; I felt out of place within its walls.

Now, as a young woman, I longed more than ever for the freedom to not have decisions made for me. As a woman in the U.S. I knew I would be free—free to be fully educated, to pursue my dreams wherever they would take me, to marry the man I wanted to marry. If I had to return to Iran for a few years to teach, as I assumed would happen, I would not be the same person. Even if I found freedom for only a few years, I would never give it up again.

It was time to board my flight. I said my final goodbyes, picked up my luggage, and walked out onto tarmac with the other passengers. A tumult of emotions cascaded through me, yet I maintained the same calm and outward demeanor that had carried me through all my family's hardships and tragedies. There were no tears.

At the top of the steps to the plane I turned back to wave. I stored my luggage and took a seat with three other women who had won scholarships. My sadness was gone. I felt elated now, as if I was being liberated. While I was afraid of flying for the first time, I had no fear about the journey I was about to make. As I sat back and the plane prepared for takeoff, I did not know where I was going or what I would find, but I was ready to embrace and accept whatever the future would bring.

One

In my earliest childhood memory, poetry and music are seamlessly intertwined. I was a very young child when my parents took me to visit their various friends. Until well past midnight, the hostess entertained us with musicians, poetry recitals, and plenty of food. My father Haibatullah was a man immersed in the history of Persia, and he thought his children should be exposed to the history and culture of the country from a very young age.

I didn't want to be there. It was very difficult to sit still amid the adult conversation, but protesting would have been useless; in our culture, it wasn't acceptable to question our parents. We were brought up to listen to their wisdom and to learn from their experiences. And yet, while I fidgeted and longed to be home in my bed, I felt touched in some way by the poetry I heard. The words of Omar Khayyam rang in my ears:

> *Ah, make the most of what we yet may spend,*
> *Before we too into Dust descend;*
> *Dust into Dust, and under Dust, to Lie,*
> *Sans Wine, sans song, sans Singer, and—sans End!*

Soon I became drowsy from the sounds of the violins and curled up next to my mother. When it came time to leave, I had to be led by the hand for a drowsy walk through the dark streets of our town. In the days and years that followed, I realized that the poetry I heard that night had become a part of me in a way I couldn't understand or explain; the meaning of the lyrics had escaped me, but I somehow understood them in a way that went deeper than mere words. It was my first taste of the beauty of Persian culture, an appreciation that has lasted all my life.

Soon I was reciting poetry in elementary school, and I heard it read aloud at picnics, weddings, birthday parties, funerals, and on the streets. It was as much a part of the texture of our lives as the landscapes that surrounded us.

Outside our house were freshwater canals lined with Cyprus pine and flowering trees; people would gather in the shade and soak their feet in the cool water while they drank their tea and ate their snacks. Someone would recite a poem or two, while others played the violin, the mandolin, or tabla drums. They might dance alone or in groups (men and women didn't dance together). As a child, I understood that the pleasures of life and nature were inseparable.

Rezaiyeh, the city in far northwest of Iran where I grew up, was situated in a breathtaking landscape of green hills, rivers, and waterfalls. Due to the exquisite scenery and city architecture, it was often called "the Paris of Persia." As a child, I watched spring water from the mountains surge into a magnificent and vast freshwater river within walking distance from our home; the swirling waters, churning in a circular and synchronized fashion, reminded me of the chanting and dancing of whirling dervishes—mystical dancers from the Sufi sect of Islam.

Along the riverbank was a park with flower gardens, willow trees, and a large mulberry orchard. Overlooking the river were wildflower-covered hills bursting with small native Persian Juno Irises (*Iris Persica*) and patches of scarlet Asian poppies that mingled with silvery blue echinops. Beyond the lush hills was a mountain carpeted with dark gorse and fragrant bushes nestled under cedars and low-growing oaks. In the distance was a shepherd with a flock of grazing sheep and goats; he was waving his staff like he was dancing.

Most evenings my family and I would take a walk to the park along the river, passing cultivated fields of wheat, corn, barley, and fruit trees. We would stop at the well-stocked roadside farm, purchase fresh green cucumbers wrapped in burlap, and carry them to the park to eat like fruit. To this day, I still prepare the meals of my childhood for my family—cucumber mixed with yogurt and mint, or a salad of chopped cucumber, tomato, basil, and onion.

Some days we continued our leisurely walk to the park's mulberry tree orchard. It was a very popular place; among the trees were picnic tables for families to sit and enjoy the fresh berries. We watched a young man climb the tree and shake the fruit onto a large, white canvas cloth spread below. The berries were sold on round copper trays the size of a large pizza pan. My older sister Pooran and I dressed for the park in tailored skirts, blouses, and a pretty pinafore, just like we were going to a party. The park attendants gave us smocks to shield our clothing from the purple juices of the intensely sweet berries that ran down our chins and stained our fingers.

Our house in Rezaiyeh was located on Pahlavi Avenue, the main avenue in our town that was named after the Shah. It ran north to south through the center of the city, a wide street with spacious walkways along both sides. Across the street was a drugstore owned by my uncle's brother-in-law and a block away was a cinema. A bar and restaurant next door, owned by an Assyrian family, served typical Persian food: rice, kabobs, stuffed grape leaves (dolma), and famous Iranian herb soup with yogurt. Because Assyrians were Christian, they could legally serve alcohol and homemade wine in their establishments but Muslims could not. On the next block was a small store that brought in fresh produce daily; next to it was a bakery that opened its doors at four o'clock in the morning. Our household helper would leave very early to bring us bread and rolls for breakfast.

I can still remember waking to the smells of that breakfast—fresh baked thin flatbread (called lavash), feta cheese, aged blue cheese, fresh butter, and homemade cherry, quince, and rosebud jams. And always tea brewing in the samovar, an ornate brass urn of boiling water with a spigot in front. It was heated by charcoal in a tube in its center. The teapot on top held the heated water and Indian tea leaves. There is a tradition that exists to this day: when you visit a Persian home or business, tea is always offered as understood hospitality. I never drank American coffee before I came to the United States. We drank Turkish coffee to stay awake during our arduous final exams at school. Sometimes we drank coffee in social gatherings, where our friends had a tradition of reading the future in the patterns of the coffee grounds in the bottom of our cups. A bird-like shape meant that good news was on the way. I remember vividly when my good friend read my coffee cup a year before I came to the U.S. She saw the shape of a beautiful horse in my cup, meaning that I would be going far away. I was doubtful of this prediction.

I can still recall every corner of our family home, which had been a wedding gift to my parents from my paternal grandfather, a very progressive thinker. He believed newlyweds should lead independent lives and make their own decisions. It was unusual in the 1920s and 30s for young couples in Iran to live on their own; newlyweds customarily lived with their parents, grandparents, and grandchildren under one roof, usually with the groom's family. The mother-in-law and father-in-law oversaw the household, and the mother-in-law taught the daughter-in-law her family's traditions and way of life.

We had two homes joined together, designed in the fashion of 18th century architecture. The main house had a big entrance on Pahlavi Avenue. A guesthouse in back was connected to it and had its own separate entrance. The entrance door of the main house was made of redwood and metal, and there were two knockers: a heavier one for a gentleman and a lighter one for ladies that directed them to separate quarters. When male guests arrived, a household servant would accompany them to the guesthouse to be entertained. Women would rarely visit that house. Instead, they would be brought to the reception room where a female helper accompanied them to the main house. Later on, my mother installed a very simple and beautiful wooden door with a single knocker within reach of children.

After entering the front door, you stepped down into a large sunken waiting room with a high ceiling and white, bare cement walls. There was a Persian kilim covering the floor (a thin, woven, durable rug in a colorful paisley pattern), and two long benches with cushions along both walls.

On the second floor a hallway divided two large living areas. One was the formal reception room for guests, with French red velvet brocade furniture and walls covered with oriental rugs. On the other side of the hallway were my family's quarters, divided into a living room and bedrooms. All the children slept in one bedroom, my parents had the other bedroom, and there was also a sitting room and an enclosed balcony. Downstairs was the kitchen and a separate storage room that also doubled as a playroom.

Every room in my parents' house was covered with Persian rugs and carpets. Persian carpets depict history, nature, and art, are usually made of very fine wool or a combination of silk and wool, and are colored with natural dyes. These carpets were found on the floors, on the walls as decoration, and sometimes on the streets. In our reception room hung a carpet that depicted the landscape of the desert; emerging from this seemingly desolate background were wildflowers, trees, and the blossoming greens of early spring. We also had a garden carpet that depicted a 17th century hunting scene and the palace of Cyrus the Great, with water flowers, fish, and wild animals among the almond, Cyprus, and plane trees.

I remember so well the special carpet that hung on our living room wall, depicting a person's journey in life from infancy to old age. During one of his trips abroad my father brought home a replica of an ancient Persian rug that had my sister's name on it: Poorandukht. The original rug is in the Hermitage Museum in St. Petersburg, Russia and is considered a great treasure. It tells the seventh century story of two sisters of the king of Persia,

6

A Checkerboard of Nights and Days

Azarmidukht and Poorandukht, who became ministers after their brother's death, evidence that women in Persian history held important positions in the kingdom. When I got married my mother sent me two beautiful Kashan carpets that I still have in my house today, and they still look brand new. There is an old saying that Persian ladies are durable like Persian carpets—you can walk on them but they never get worn.

There is, however, one place that is especially embedded in my memory, that I dream about more often these days—the courtyard in the center of our home where we spent so much of our lives in every season. The courtyard was our private sanctuary, surrounded by nine-foot brown clay walls and full of life.

We would sit in the garden, breathe in the fresh air, and enjoy the heavenly aroma of the flowers—roses, pansies, begonias, gladiolas, anemones, irises, and jasmines. We grew basil, leeks, parsley, green onion, and a variety of mint, using the herbs in soups and stews, for medicine, or drying them for their aromas. There was an oasis of fruit trees in our courtyard—plum, pear, peach, apple, apricot, persimmon, flowering almond, and a sour cherry tree that towered above us. In the center of the courtyard was a freshwater pool fed with spring water from the mountains above Rezaiyeh via underground pipes. Very early in the morning our maid Jayran would collect all the fresh water needed for the day in large containers, which we would use for making tea, cooking, watering the garden, and bathing.

When I woke up I would wash my face in the water of the pool; it was so clear and pure that I could see the pebbles at the bottom. I played in the courtyard all day with my siblings and our friends, swam in the pool in the sweltering summer months, and picked flowers, herbs, and vegetables for dinner.

When my brothers Manoochehr and Bahman climbed the tall cherry tree in the garden, my mother would get worried and tell them, "You come down right now! You've climbed far too high!" Bahman would sit in the top branches, dangling his feet and singing like a bird.

That tree provided us with so much fruit, which we used to make cherry jam and cherry drinks. I remember the rushing sounds of the nuthatches, rose finches, and sparrows as they came to feed, scattering pits on the courtyard stones. Beyond the tree was an outhouse; the toilet was a hole in the ground and a watering can served as a bidet. It was such a pain to use it at night. A fanous (an old-fashioned light) was hung above the door for when we used it at night. Later the outhouse was changed into a more modern facility.

Our lives revolved around our garden, the joy of which stays with me today. We ate our breakfast at a square wooden table located in the middle of it; only in the winter would we eat inside the house. Our living room had a large window looking out upon it, so we were never far from its beauty even when inside. Most Iranian families had beautiful gardens. Persians created gardens 2,500 years ago, which they called "Paradise on Earth." Poets continually wrote about gardens. During the Islamic Empire, they became a place for sacred contemplation and spiritual nourishment. All flowers in the Persian language are called gole; roses are called red gole and are considered the mother of all flowers. Iranians use rosewater for everything—body cream, perfume, ice cream, sherbet, cookies, and oil. When guests arrive for weddings and special occasions, you welcome them by pouring rosewater on their hands.

In the words of the poet Hafez Shirazi:

The soft murmur of the breeze will pour forth its music;
The old world will find youth anew, the Judas tree will offer
Its purple cup to jasmine. As the eye of the narcissus gazes
At the anemone, after the long sorrow of exile,
The warbling nightingale will take flight to the shelter of the rose.

When we left Rezaiyeh so I could attend the university in Tabriz, I missed my home and its garden terribly, reminding me of another poem by Rumi:

Listen to the reed how it tells a tale,
Complaining of a separation
Saying: "Ever since I was parted from the
Reed bed, my lament has caused man
And woman to moan...."

On summer nights, we slept on the roof of our house. We lay down on straw mattresses covered with Persian paisley cotton sheets, gazing up at the still blue sky that slowly darkened to reveal a glittering, diamond-studded universe. The night sky was so vast and mysterious to a young child. Two blocks away was an outdoor movie house that played Arabic and Turkish movies, and from our rooftop vantage point we caught glimpses of the scenes unfolding, of men riding white stallions on crowded streets, and the cool breeze carried the sounds of the music and dialogue to our ears.

Catching snippets of the movies was a special treat for me and my older sister Pooran because at that time our parents did not allow us girls to attend movies. Once my friend and I slipped into the movie theater, covering our faces so the ticket taker wouldn't recognize us. My parents weren't happy when they found out.

My mother Simonzare came from a family of landowners, people who weren't highly educated but were well off. My maternal grandparents were very hard workers who took care of their farms and farmers. When my mother was young she was engaged to someone in my grandmother's family, but she didn't want to marry into that family because of their lack of education. My mother had only four years of elementary school because my grandmother thought that was enough. My mother wasn't happy that she couldn't continue her education, but that's how it was for women in Iran at that time.

Both my paternal and maternal grandfathers belonged to the Baha'i faith, but my grandmothers belonged to the Muslim faith. The Baha'i faith later spread through Iran during the country's modernization period. My mother accepted the Baha'i faith as a young woman, and she became involved in that community and met my father at a Baha'i social gathering. She broke off her previous engagement and decided to marry my father. Her Muslim mother didn't agree with it, but luckily her father gave permission. It was very unusual for a young lady at that time to choose her future husband, as most marriages were arranged between families.

A Checkerboard of Nights and Days

When they married, my father was working in a telegram office, a very modern technology at that time. After their first child, Alládin, a son, was born, my grandfather urged my father to complete his education. When my father left to study biology and science for two years at Tehran University, my brother and mother went to live with my mother's parents. My father trained to be a doctor. We never knew exactly what his specialty was because he cared for farm animals as well as people. He might have been trained as a veterinarian. He was well educated in literature, science, and politics. When he returned to Rezaiyeh he was the only doctor there and was employed by the government. His friends affectionately called him "Doc Babi."

Eventually my parents had five children: Alládin, Pooran, me, Manoochehr, and Bahman.

My father named me Irandukht ("daughter of Iran") because he loved his country. Persian names are very cultural. Daughters are named after flowers or queens, and sons are named after kings and historical men. However, religious people named their children after prophets and prophets' family members. Girls were named Fatima and Khadija; boys were named Mohammad, Hussain, and Ali.

I have a photo of my mother when she was expecting her first child. She is seated in a chair; my father stands next to her in a suit with a vest. My father's younger brother stands to the right of my mother. It's a beautiful photo; my mother wears a dark dress with a large white ribbon on the bodice and clutches a purse in her lap; my father has dark blonde hair, a stern gaze, and holds his hands behind his back. Their westernized clothing is the way most men and women dressed in Iran until the 1979 Islamic revolution. With their dark hair and complexions and serene gazes, my parents could be mistaken for an Italian immigrant couple newly arrived on Ellis Island.

Two

Rezaiyeh was a very diverse city located in the far northwest of Iran in the province of Azerbaijan. It was known for centuries as Uroomia ("in between two mountains") until Reza Shah, the King and founder of the Pahlavi dynasty, named it Rezaiyeh after himself. After the revolution in 1979, the Islamic Republic reinstated the city's old name, but I call it Rezaiyeh because that is how I remember it, the beautiful city of my youth. Located not far from the borders of Iraq, Turkey, and southern Russia, it was a melting pot that stood for centuries at the crossroads of multiple cultures and civilizations. The Alborz and Azerbaijan mountains loom in the distance, and the soil, colored fawn and silver, is saturated with minerals and salt.

The word "Azerbaijan" brings to mind a determined people with strong character, colorful clothes, tambourines, and sword dances. It is a country of woolen blankets, coats made of goatskin, and ancient bazaars. The region has a long, turbulent history with many revolutions and military occupations. Areas of the state were very tribal and isolated from the rest of the country by impenetrable mountain ranges, steep valleys, and long, cold winters.

Rezaiyeh provided me with a rare multi-cultural experience based on acceptance and harmony. The city's atmosphere of diversity and inclusion had a profound effect on me, shaping my entire life. Our neighbors were Armenians, Assyrians, Turks, Kurds, Jews, and Iranian natives, who lived side by side without conflict. They worshipped their faith in churches, synagogues, and mosques. One fourth of the city's population was not Muslim and they were included in all professions—farmers, doctors, engineers, artisans, musicians, teachers, and government employees. This minority group considered themselves Persian, having settled in the area centuries ago.

Armenians have lived in Iran for a very long time, and the magnificent 11th century Christian monastery in Rezaiyeh is proof of this. To this day, they have a pastoral celebration every year. An ancient and dilapidated Christian church still stands on the Iranian side of the Aras River and is open to visitors. Jewish people have also lived in Iran for centuries; some were our neighbors and many lived in the city of Hamadan; they assimilated into Persian society, becoming an inseparable part of the country. In Rezaiyeh everyone socialized with everyone else, except for the conservative Muslims who lived in a separate part of the city and kept mostly to themselves.

Nellie Sarkazian, my childhood friend from kindergarten, was Assyrian and she taught me a lot about her culture. Most Assyrians (also called Ashouri or Ashuri) are Christians and speak the Aramaic language; they are a Semitic and Mediterranean ethnic people. Nellie lived within walking distance from me with her grandmother, parents, and brother in a lovely house with a magical garden. She was a very bright girl who was excellent in math and later studied business at the University of Tehran.

A Checkerboard of Nights and Days

Assyrian food was completely different from what our family ate as it was much more western. They had special Assyrian sweets and rice pudding, and ate a lot of stuffed cabbage. Once they invited me for Easter dinner and that is how I learned about all of the Christian celebrations.

Our next-door neighbors were very strict Muslims and never left their house. Sometimes my siblings and I tried to peer into their compound from our rooftop. They didn't have a pretty garden like we did. The lady of the house never showed her face, but at times we saw the other women of the house covered entirely with the chador, a full-length, loose covering made of cotton or silk, usually black, that enveloped their bodies from head to toe. It's normally held in place by pinching together the fabric under the chin with your hand and is worn over dresses.

My part of town was populated with many refugees, which is how I met an Armenian named Mervat, better known to us as "Mamma Bozork." Her name derived from her heavyset build and gentle, motherly nature. She made a delicious Armenian sweet called nazook or gatab— a sweetbread of puffed dough stuffed with honey and nuts. When we went on picnics together she brought along these wonderful sweets.

Mamma Bozork introduced us to her culture not only through food, but through stories of the horrors she survived. She was a refugee from the Armenian Genocide of 1915-17, when the Ottoman Turks systematically killed more than 1.5 million Armenians. Her husband died in the slaughter, and she escaped to Rezaiyeh by travelling on foot for hundreds of miles with her young son and daughter. My mother befriended her and they became very close, the best friend that I can remember my mother having. She came to visit us often.

Mamma Bozork was a fortune teller who also read the future in the sediment left behind in cups of Turkish coffee. She was a lot of fun. Later she moved to Tabriz, and when we also moved to that city in 1950 she let us stay in her small guest house until we found a place to live. Her children were musicians and entertained us in their main home. This family was a wonderful part of our life. Mamma Bozork was so warm and motherly that I feel she is still with me.

During my childhood, I was fortunate to be surrounded by a lot of very strong and kind women. One was Madam Andranic, who belonged to the Armenian Church and was our closest neighbor in Rezaiyeh. She and her husband were excellent tailors; she made dresses while he made suits and coats. After my father died, we couldn't pay for a tailor to make clothes for my mother, my sister, and me, so one summer I asked Madam Andranic if she would teach me to sew.

She responded, "I will be very happy to teach you. I don't want any money, but I would ask that you teach mathematics to my nine-year-old son because he just doesn't understand it." I told her I would be very happy to do so.

I learned everything from her: how to sew, how to knit, how to do needlework. Every day I went to her house and sewed clothes for my mother, sister, brother, and myself. Madam Andranic taught me well with a great deal of kindness and patience. When I went away to college, she made me a beautiful suit and shirt that I wore often to my classes. When my sister Pooran got married she made me a lovely dress and wouldn't charge me for it. I don't sew much nowadays, but whenever I do I always remember her telling me that if you're tired and frustrated, leave your work, rest, and then start again.

When I was just five years old, I loved to carry a basket into our courtyard gardens and pick a variety of herbs—basil, parsley, green onion, coriander, and watercress. I called it "sabad pora, sabzi khordani" ("my basketful of herbs"). I took them to the dining room to be eaten with lunch, as it was customary in Iranian culture to eat herbs instead of salad with main meals. My nickname was "kufta gal galee" (little moving meatball), given to me by my uncle because I was short and round. My relatives would pull on my cheeks affectionately whenever they called me by my nickname.

An appreciation for food and its preparation was a central part of our culture. Iranian tradition was to have bread with every meal. For breakfast, we ate thin bread called lavosh, and a longer and thicker bread called sangak. We ate feta and blue cheese with the bread, along with homemade jam, butter, and a very heavy and rich yogurt.

Lunch was the main meal of the day, usually consisting of ab-goosht, a lamb stew with fresh tomatoes and green peppers simmered for hours in a clay pot, or soup made with a variety of herbs and greens, such as spinach, cilantro, parsley, chives, and garlic, and topped with yogurt. We also ate a salad with mint, cucumber, and garlic, and another salad with tomato, onion, green pepper, and cucumbers. Sometimes we would have eggplant stew and zucchini stew with beef for lunch. In the summer, we would barbeque kabobs over a charcoal pit and serve them with plenty of basmati rice, accompanied by a basketful of herbs.

Around four in the afternoon we enjoyed tea time with biscuits, jam, and sweets. In the early evening, we'd eat a very light dinner of bread, a simple soup, cheese, yogurt, vegetables, and a cucumber salad.

We always ate fruit after dinner, depending on what was in season. In the fall, we ate grapes with cheese and bread. We would have sweets and desserts only on special occasions, such as the Persian New Year, weddings, and big parties, but never with meals. And of course, we drank lots of very sweet tea. We even gave tea to babies. To this day, I still drink tea with a sugar cube in my mouth.

I spent many delightful summers with my family vacationing at famous Rezaiyeh Lake (now known as Uroomia Lake), a turquoise-colored gem that was fed by snow and rainwater from the nearby mountains. We floated effortlessly in the heavily salted water, which made it easy to learn how to swim; the lake supplied enough salt for the entire country. Camped by the turquoise waters of Uroomia Lake, the landscape of my childhood seemed like a paradise.

When we were very young, before we had a car, we would travel there by horse and buggy with our supplies. We pitched a tent and stayed for three days. We dug a pit in the sand, collected wood, and built a fire for barbeques and cooking. Sometimes other picnickers shared their fires with us. The aroma of roasted meat, corn, and vegetables filled the air (along with the smell of hashish, which some men smoked because it was legal). The lake was surrounded by salt pillars that looked like the forlorn columns of ancient ruined temples; we climbed those pillars. Our Armenian friends shared their delicate sweets, snacks, and tea with us. We loved their sweetbread so much that later my mother learned how to bake it, although it was a very long process. I have the recipe from my Armenian classmate, but haven't made it recently because of the complicated recipe. When I visit my daughter Randa in Washington D.C., I buy it from an Armenian bakery called Mama Lavash.

Rezaiyeh, with a climate like southern California's, was famous for producing wine from ten different kinds of grapes. The area was also known for raisins and concentrated grape syrup, which was used to make sweets like rice pudding and halva.

One of my most vivid memories as a young child is visiting my maternal grandparents' home in Rezaiyeh. They lived in a compound of three connected homes that occupied the whole street. Like everyone in my family they spoke both the Azari language, a dialect of Turkish, because of their Azerbaijani heritage, as well as the official language of my country (Farsi). Written with the Arabic alphabet, Azari is a mixture of Indo-European and Semitic languages.

A courtyard was between two of their buildings; in the middle of it was a tanur or pit oven, about five feet deep and made of clay. The opening was about three feet wide and shaped like a crooked circle. The bottom of the tanur was filled with coal that made a red-hot fire to heat the walls of the pit. When I was only four or five years old I loved to watch flatbread (lavash) being baked.

Irandukht Vahidi Fahmy

The bakers were two young girls with round faces, red cheeks, and braided long hair tied with scarves. They would arrive the night before from their nearby village to prepare the dough for the bread. Their names were Zohreh and Sakinea, and their job was to bake enough bread to feed my parents, siblings, and two uncles for the next few months. Zohreh and Sakinea awoke at five a.m. to start baking all day and into the night. They sat across from each other; one would roll the dough on a large stone until it was very thin. The other girl then slapped the dough, about the size of a pizza, against the walls of the tanur. There was no fire or smoke, just heat to bake the bread. Sometimes they allowed me to roll dough into round balls before they flattened it on the stone.

I watched as the bread baked to a toasted brown, bubbled on top from the heat. They picked it from the oven with their bare hands and piled it on thick cotton cloth, sprayed it with water, and covered it with more cloth to keep it from drying out. Somehow the bread remained fresh and dry for many days in storage; for several months we would eat it with every meal.

The smell of hot bread and watching it being baked made me so happy. I would ask Zohreh and Sakinea for a piece of dough. Then I'd make a ball out of it and they would bake it for me. I would run to my grandmother crying, "Give me cheese and butter for my hot bread!" The cheese was what we call Farmer's cheese today. Watching the bakers bake, eating the cheese with warm bread, being with my family and grandparents—those were some of my happiest times.

Zohreh and Sakinea belonged to a religion called Ali-Illahi, a sect of Shia Islam that believes Ali, the son-in-law of the prophet

Mohammed, is God. It was a secret sect, more mystical than Sunnis or Shia, and neither of the girls ever talked much about it.

They wore loose, baggy pants (called shalwar) that tapered to a tight fit around the ankles, and tops with three-quarter length sleeves. Their long, dark-brown hair was braided; scarves patterned in paisley were wrapped around their heads and tied at the crown to protect them from the heat.

My grandmother had special rooms attached to the main house where the bakers slept. Next to the baker's room there was a storage room filled with bread, raisins, wheat buds, and nuts to be sold at the market, and other supplies that their helpers loaded on donkeys and brought from the village. The fun part was that my cousins and I would go and fill our pockets with the various nuts and raisins, and share them with our friends.

Memories of the food we ate remain with me until today. An Assyrian woman named Maryam lived three hours away on a farm where they raised sheep and goats. She was tall and muscular with a friendly, open face. She would make fresh yogurt overnight—thick, Greek-like yogurt. In the morning she covered it with a thick cloth and carried the large container on her head to reach our house by seven a.m. with the freshest, most delicious yogurt I have ever eaten. My mother would give her raisins, sugar, and nuts for her children. Marian used the money she made from selling yogurt to buy food in town for her family.

B ibi Ghazee was another strong and important woman in my life; stocky with dark brown skin and short red hair, she was somehow related to my maternal grandmother. She and her husband oversaw my grandparents' village and made sure every-thing was in order. When my mother married, Bibi Ghazee ac-companied her to the newlywed home, an Iranian tradition in well-to-do families, where an older woman wise in the ways of the world taught the bride about sexuality, how to treat her husband, and how to manage a household.

We looked forward to Bibi's visits because she brought along colorful candies and grape syrup as thick as honey. She was larg-er than life, very bossy, and we loved her, especially because she believed in spirits, genies, and gypsies, and told us stories about them. She said that gypsies lived in tents, and moved about in search of water and food for themselves and their animals. They made beautiful artifacts for sale.

She would often sleep over in the female helper's room in-stead of walking back to the village, and we would keep Bibi up at night so she could tell us her stories—*One Thousand and One Nights,* old Persian tales, and stories about my grandparents. We were enchanted as we sat on the roof with her, staring at the stars as we imagined the kings and queens of ancient times. But Bibi also scared us, telling us that a genie would come and take us away from our family if we didn't listen to her.

As she wove her stories and kept us entranced, she constantly chewed a black gummy substance, which I later learned was a mix-ture of poppy seeds and Arabic gum. My mother explained to me: "She boils the seeds of poppy flowers and makes a hard jelly and chews it. It's a drug and Bibi is addicted."

This "poppy seed jelly" was readily available in her village and all over Iran at the time. An uncle of mine who was the family poet was also addicted. He would openly smoke this form of opium at family picnics while reciting his favorite poetic verse. When our family went to Lake Rezaiyeh for family outings, townspeople (including army and police officers) would sit around the charcoal stove and smoke hashish in long pipes.

Sadly, Bibi Ghazee later died from complications associated with addiction, when I was living in the United States; Pooran sent me a very sad letter that she had passed on. I still remember her round face, big eyes, and reddish hair.

Three

From Bibi's stories, I learned so much about my culture and history. Even today Iranians are much more interested in Persian history than in modern day Iran. For me, to this day, Iran is Persia. For most westerners, knowledge of Iran starts and ends with the 1979 Islamic Revolution. Americans in particular have a very narrow and monolithic view of Iran, formed by the 1980 hostage crisis that played out during the Carter Administration. Few know that, before the revolution, the country was entirely different from how it is today, and that Persia is an ancient, complex civilization with great achievements.

When I was growing up, my country of birth was a combination of Islamic and Zoroastrian culture. The Islamic invaders brought their religion and the Arabic language, but we spoke Persian (Farsi) growing up, not Arabic. I grew up with the Baha'i faith, which was somewhat different from the Islamic faith. Our calendar, holidays, and even our language came from an ancient Zoroastrian culture, which was the first known state religion of Persia, dating to the first century B.C.

Zoroastrianism believes in two opposite elements, the angel and the devil, with their god Ahura-Mazda (the God of Light) representing and creating all that is good. Zoroastrianism believes that an evil spirit named Ahriman crashed through the sky, punched down through the oceans, and burst into the center of the earth, creating mountains and rivers. Thus, began the struggle between the opposing elements of good and evil, light and dark.

Zoroastrianism is a simple faith with a simple credo: it worships nature and light. The Zoroastrian faith influenced the course of Shi'ism, a mystical school of thought. Shi'ism later became the official religion of the country during the Safavid dynasty. Both religions believed that light constitutes a symbolic reminder of the spiritual in the natural world. A visit to prominent Shia shrines, mosques, and palaces in Iran reveals the importance of light with their luminous rooms of cut metalwork and windows carved skillfully to reflect light from all angles. Light affects the psychological mood and wellbeing of human beings. It is well known that in countries with less daylight, it has been proven that there is more depression and suicide among their people.

The Zoroastrians stood for good thinking, good speaking, and good behavior, and believed in the three elements of nature: fire, water, and air. Their calendar was based on the movement of the sun, which they believed would be victorious over darkness. They burned fires all night long to insure defeat for the forces of Ahriman. Daytime marked the victory of the sun over darkness and was celebrated as a festival on the first day of each month, featuring a feast, acts of charity, and honoring deities. Plays were performed to insure the total victory of the sun, which was essential for the protection of winter crops. There were prayers to Mithra, a deity responsible for the light of the early morning and for protecting people. It was also assumed that Ahura-Mazda would grant people's wishes, especially to children with no parents.

One theme of the festival was a temporary subversion of order. Masters and servants would reverse their roles; the king dressed in white and changed places with ordinary people. Rules of living were relaxed and people celebrated with joy. Candles and lamps chased away the darkness and allowed light to prevail.

Some Zoroastrians still practice these traditions in the small villages of Iran, but most left the country because of Islamic persecution and settled in India where they are called Parsees. One of the traditions they still practice is to put the bodies of deceased people on their roofs and let the birds consume them.

The most cherished of all Persian festivals is the Persian New Year ("Nowruz," or "New Day"), which has been celebrated for 2,500 years and is rooted in the Zoroastrian worship of nature. Another ancient but vital Zoroastrian tradition is to celebrate the first night of Winter, Dec. 21, the longest and darkest night of the year; the holiday is called Shab e Yelda in honor of the birth of the Sun God who symbolizes light, goodness, and strength in the ultimate triumph over darkness. During Shab e Yelda families gather together to celebrate and read poetry, as in these lines by Saadi Shirazi:

Like all my pain, there is still the hope of recovery,
Like the eve of Yelda, there will finally be an end.
After winter night of Shab e Yelda, a transformation takes place,
The waiting is over, light shines, and goodness prevails.
The sight of you each morning is the New Year. And the night
Of departure is the eve of Yelda.

A Checkerboard of Nights and Days

While we recited poetry, fires were burning outside our house. As a child, I would see young people jumping over a fire for good luck. It was an old Persian New Year and Yelda tradition, like farm festivals and winter festivals in the United States.

Our tables would be laden with watermelon, pomegranate, and grapes; the red of the watermelon and pomegranate symbolized the hues of dawn and the glow of life. We ate walnuts, almonds, and ajeel, a mixture of nuts, roasted chick peas, several kinds of raisins, figs, sunflower seeds, and dates.

It was a tradition to make a wish and then open a poetry book to a random page and read the first poem to find out whether or not the wish would come true. It was also customary for grandparents to tell stories to their grandchildren during the night. Everyone would sit around a low table called a corsi that was covered with quilts and blankets. A small charcoal fire under the corsi radiated heat through the blankets and into the room. There were four mattresses on each side of the table; as children, we would stretch out on the mattresses and cover up with quilts as the corsi kept us warm, listening to our grandparents and Bibi Ghazee telling us stories as we snacked on fruits, nuts, cookies, and tea.

The story that I heard most often was *One Thousand and One Nights, also* known as *The Arabian Nights.* We loved hearing the story of King Shahryar of Persia who was so distraught by his wife's infidelity that he killed her and convinced himself that all women were deceitful. His great revenge was that he would marry a new wife every night and murder her the next morning. Until Scheherazade came along and told him stories every night

– for 1001 nights - stopping just short on the conclusion of the story, so he wouldn't murder her. We loved the story because it portrayed a strong, clever, and empowered woman as the real hero.

Iranian Jews, who were among the oldest inhabitants of the country, and some of whom were our neighbors, celebrated both Shab e Yelda and Birkat Ha'llanot, the festival of the blessing of the trees. They lit candles, ate dried and fresh fruit, prepared special meals, and performed prayers.

My family had a special reason for celebrating Shab e Yelda, for I arrived in the world at two a.m. on Dec. 21, 1932, with the help of Khadijeh, a Muslim midwife, both of my grandmothers, and Bibi Ghazee. I was born small but healthy, and was immediately wrapped in blankets and placed in a room next to my mother's bedroom.

That night there were many fire pits in the streets and young girls were jumping over them, wishing for good husbands and good marriages. There was much singing and dancing around the fires. Men had sheepskin blankets on their shoulders and the ladies wore red, blue, and cream colored shawls to protect them from the dry cold. While the dancing went on, people ate whole pomegranates and chewed the seeds.

While everyone became distracted by fireworks being set off to celebrate Shab e Yelda, I lay face down on the mattress for more than ten minutes; my nose became flattened and I had trouble breathing. My mother cried out "Where's my baby!? Check on the baby!" Bibi Ghazee ran in, picked me up, and slapped me into breathing normally. According to Zoroastrian and Persian tradition, a woman should be at a baby's side for ten days to protect the mother and child from the "evil eye," which is exactly what Bibi did. She said an evil-eyed genie must have been in the house.

She made sure my mother was rested and fed very rich food, such as halava, a special sweet made of flour, honey, butter, and saffron. In those days being thin was a sign of poverty; it was desirable for a woman to be plump.

After the ten-day protective period was over and the evil eye could no longer harm the baby, visitors were allowed to see my mother and me. Every day, friends and family visited with their children. Cups of hot tea, plenty of cookies, and ajeel in large colorful dishes was served from morning to night.

Pooran was three years old when I was born. She wore a pretty dress for the guests who were arriving to see the newborn baby. Her long golden hair fell down her back and she wore a beautiful white bone European comb in her hair as a decoration. My paternal grandmother Kokeb Khanoum and Pooran resembled each other and were very close. "Poori Joon," my grandmother said, "you have a little sister!"

Pooran looked at me and decided I needed something for my thick, short, black hair. She snapped her comb in two and said, "Half for me, half for my sister!" Pooran displayed that kind of generosity her entire life.

Sadly, with the Muslim conquest of Persia, most of the culture and traditions of ancient Persia were lost.

The beginning of Islam can be traced to Muhammed's birth in Mecca, Saudi Arabia in 570. Although Muhammed was a merchant, he was known for his deep spirituality ability to communicate God's word. In 610, Muhammed climbed a mountain and entered a cave to pray. He was in deep prayer when an angel visited him and delivered a message from God. Muhammed then began to recite these messages, believing they were directly from God. He gathered these revelation into one book, The Holy Qur'an, and quickly gained followers. The Islamic faith began to rapidly spread throughout the continent of Arabia.

When the Prophet Muhammad died, there was a disagreement over who should succeed him. Muhammad never named his successor, so his cousin/brother-in-law Ali stepped up and self-proclaimed that he was the successor. However, the followers of Muhammed insisted that the leaders of the Islamic Council should choose a successor democratically. The Islamic Council convened and chose Abu-Bakr, a wise and learned confidant of Muhammed to succeed him. Thus, the beginnings of the deepest schism in Islam. The followers of Abu-Bakr became the Sunni sect of Islam, and those that insisted Ali was their leader became the Shia sect.

But the schism did not end there. Tensions rose between Sunni and Shia giving rise to the first Islamic civil war. As the battle raged on, Ali was eventually killed and his son, Husain stepped up to succeed him. Husain insisted on continuing the civil war, primarily to seek revenge for this father's death. However Husain also perished in the war, and his successor continued the battle, spreading Shi'ism throughout the region including to the Persian Empire.

A Checkerboard of Nights and Days

Initially when Islam spread to the Persian Empire, the kings took advantage of the schism and adopted Shi'ism as a political maneuver, in essence a way to distinguish Persian culture from Arab culture. They viewed the Sunni sect as too focused on Arab culture and traditions. But by the time the Safavid Dynasty (1501-1799 A.D.) began in Iran, Shi'ism became the official proclaimed religion. The religious leaders (Imams) gained power and slowly began to replace Persian culture, institutions and buildings, with Islamic religious institutions and mosques. Many Persians fled to other countries during this period, but some remained behind desperately trying to save their culture, including Shab e Yelda, the celebration of the first day of winter, and Nowruz, the first day of spring.

Despite the Sunni Shia divide, the fundamental tenants of Islam have endured many centuries. Muslims believe in one God and the Prophet Muhammad is his messenger. Every Muslim must follow the five most important pillars of the religion: the declaration of faith with one God and Muhammad as his messenger; the Hajj: pilgrimage to the holy place of Mecca, Saudi Arabia; Zakat: the practice of charity; fasting for 30 days from sunrise to sundown during the holy month of Ramadan; and prayer five times a day.

Today, Iran has the largest population of Shia Muslims in the world. Other countries with Shia majority populations are: Iraq, Bahrain, Azerbaijan, and Yemen. The majority of Sunnis reside in Saudi Arabia, Indonesia, Turkey, Jordan, and Egypt. Many of the current sectarian wars occurring in the Middle East, especially in Iraq and Syria, are between Shia and Sunni Muslims.

Irandukht Vahidi Fahmy

The 1979 Islamic Revolution in Iran helped propel the religious leaders, who follow the most extreme interpretations of Shi'ism, back into power. They control all political, economic and religious aspects of the country. Similar to what occurred during the Safavid Dynasty, these leaders have tried to discourage Persian cultural holidays including Shab e Yelda and Nowruz.

Four

The major traumatic experience of my childhood was the loss of my ten-year-old brother Alládin in 1937, when I was in kindergarten. His name meant "God is my judge" in Arabic, but his nickname was Aloosh.

When I came home from school around noon, I loved to sit in the windowsill on the second floor to gaze at the main avenue. One day at around four o'clock I noticed a commotion in front of our house. Why were people gathered there, talking and waving their hands? Why were their faces so sad? Something was very wrong but none of my instincts told me it had anything to do with my family.

A few moments later I saw my father walking quickly down the street. I ran down to the courtyard just as he came in, appearing pale and dazed. He threw his hat to the ground in the garden and shouted to my mother, "*He's gone! He's gone! He's gone!*"

My mother responded, "Who is gone?"

Our neighbors now crowded into the courtyard and embraced my mother, telling her, "God is with you! He has gone to heaven!"

At that moment my sister Pooran walked in, still in her school uniform. My mother realized that my brother wasn't with her as he always was. My grandmother cried out, "*Allah, Akbar! Allah, Akbar! God is great! God is great!*" and the women from the neighborhood began banging the palms of their hands against the sides of their heads, the sign of mourning. Yet I still had no idea what was going on.

"What did we lose?" my mother again asked my father. "What did we lose?"

"We lost our son!"

My mother fainted right in front of me as the neighbors tried to lift her up.

Why, I said to myself, *what happened?* It still didn't sink in. I watched the turmoil around me through a haze. Suddenly I realized my oldest brother was not in the house.

The tragedy began with a fight between Aloosh and a classmate when my brother refused to give him money and threw a stone at him. Enraged, the classmate knifed my brother in the upper thigh and he bled to death.

My father was called to the scene and arrived to find his son dead in front of him. I can only imagine what he felt at that moment when he realized he couldn't save his firstborn child. The knife had struck an artery, and Aloosh bled to death because there had been no one around to help him.

For the next three or four nights the neighbors gathered throughout our house. I remember the women sitting together in one of our rooms, surrounding my weeping and grief-stricken mother. My immediate family sat on the floor in the reception room and conducted a special ceremony for Aloosh. During this ceremony, shocking everyone, a woman from our neighborhood screamed, jumped up, and ran into our courtyard as we scrambled after her to find out what was happening.

My younger brother, Manoochehr, just three years old, had fallen into the garden pool; all I could see was the top of his head as he floated face down in the water. Bibi Ghazee jumped in to save him and luckily, he was alive.

The neighbors told my mother: "Be thankful—one is in heaven and the other one is saved, and now you have to think of the welfare and destiny of the remaining children. Your other children need you."

The police had immediately arrested my brother's murderer; only 12 years old, he was thrown in jail. One night Aloosh spoke to my father in a dream: "Forgive him, dad, he didn't mean it. He was just after some money. I threw a rock at him and a fight broke out."

In the words of the famous poet Hafez:

A heart born of love
Is immortal, never dead

Irandukht Vahidi Fahmy

In the book of life
So it is written, so it is said

My father wrote a long letter to the town judge stating that my family forgave the young man. He also published his letter in the local newspaper. My mother was not in favor of this decision.

She asked, "Why do you want him set free? He has to pay for what he did to our son!!"

"I must forgive him," my father told her. "He came to me in my dream and said that he didn't mean it. Please forgive him. We must forgive him. He's young. He has a life of his own ahead of him, and I don't want him to waste it because he made a mistake. Whether he's in jail or not, our son is gone. Punishing his killer will not bring him back."

My mother eventually had to accept my father's decision.

My father begged the judge to let my brother's killer go free. He was a great letter writer and I'm not surprised he convinced the authorities to let him go. They released him after three days and sent him to his parents' family in Turkey to spare us the trauma of having him close by.

It seemed entirely natural to me that my father forgave my brother's murderer. That was the kind of person he was, extremely kind-hearted and sensitive to other people's feelings. My mother once told us, "If he saw a street vendor carrying Persian rugs on his shoulder for sale, he would buy one. Not because we needed any more rugs in our house, but because he wished to lighten the man's heavy load." If my father ran into a friend or a neighbor at lunchtime, he would invite them home for my mother's special herb soup with yogurt: "My wife just made it. Why don't you come and have lunch with me?" He was kind and generous with our servants, treated everyone with respect, and gave out tips left and right.

My mother was a completely different personality, much more logical and systematic, often upset that he spent so much money. To my mother's distress my father sold our guesthouse and with the money bought a blue 1935 Ford. No one else in Rezaiyeh had a car at the time; people would come by our house to gaze at our strange moving vehicle.

My paternal grandmother, Kokeb Khanoum, had a half-sister who had a granddaughter named Arganoosh. Arganoosh grew up in Rezaiyeh and was very close to our family. I was 14 when Arganoosh got married at age 12 to a man named Kamran, the younger brother of Aloosh's killer. Our family attended this wedding and Kamran became part of our extended family.

Kamran and Arganoosh had four children, all of whom ended up living in California. When I visited my sister Pooran there in 2011, I was able to meet one of the girls. All of their children were doing well. They knew nothing of what happened to my brother and the topic was never discussed, left in the distant past where it belonged.

After my brother's death, my mother fell into a deep depression. She would sit for hours on end in the long, bench-like windowsill in our living room and just stare at the street. Our household maids would ask her questions and she wouldn't respond. She refused to go anywhere, not even to her mother's house to visit. Sometimes I would ask her a question and she would gaze at me with a blank expression. Everyone assumed she was mourning, but it went far deeper than that.

At the time, none of us knew what depression was. We didn't have a word for it in our language. As a result, none of us acknowledged my mother's grief and no one was able to give her emotional support. It is only now, with the understanding that comes from looking back years later, that I understand what she was suffering from.

My father dealt with my brother's death by burying himself in his work; he traveled a lot throughout Kurdistan for his profession. Most days he would come home very late and leave early in the morning.

Unlike my mother, he wasn't distant when he was around us. He was the same person, but we didn't see him much and he wasn't as involved in our lives as before my brother's death. My uncle once asked my father what grade his daughters were in and he couldn't answer the question. With my mother's depression and the fact that my father was travelling most of the time, we were left to be cared for by our household helpers. Pooran, who was now the oldest child after my brother's death, tried to help as much as she could. She took on a great deal of responsibility and acted as a second mother to my two younger brothers.

My family never recovered from this tragic incident. My brother's death caused a big gap between my childhood and teenage years, a void in my world that remained unfilled.

Five

In the summer of 1939 we took our most interesting family trip, a ten-day excursion to the mountains of Kurdistan. At the time my father was the private physician for Barzanie, the head of the Kurdish tribe in Iran, who would come to our home as a guest with his many wives and servants. The Kurds were always fighting for their autonomy from Iran and were allied with the Iraqi Kurds.

Barzanie dispatched six handsome young men to our home. I watched one morning as they clattered on horseback into our courtyard, so tall and strong and very healthy looking. They brought along six beautiful horses to take us to their compound at the top of the Zagros Mountains. All the guardsmen were armed with rifles.

We set off for the eight-hour journey. The first guardsman rode ahead, on the lookout for danger. My father was atop the second horse, and the third horse carried my mother and a guardsman. On the fourth horse a guardsman held my younger brother Manoochehr in his lap and my older sister Pooran rode behind him. I rode on the fifth horse, holding the guardsman's waist so tightly I was sore by the journey's end.

Irandukht Vahidi Fahmy

It was an all-day ride on a very narrow unpaved road, but for us children it was the most exciting journey. We rode up a high and narrow valley trail between two mountains and past giant boulders; in the distance, when I peered around the guard I hugged so fiercely, I saw snow-covered mountains. As we approached the Kurdistan border I vividly remember armed Kurdish soldiers on both sides of the road, ensuring that no Iranian national forces would enter their territory.

The tribal compound seemed like a palace to me. Barzanie had four wives and eighteen children, along with his mother, siblings, and their families. As soon as we arrived my mother and the children were whisked to the women's quarters, while my father was slowly and respectfully escorted to the men's quarters to be welcomed by the head of the tribe.

The Kurdish girls and women were adorned with gold necklaces and earrings, and wore colorful silk skirts and blouses with shawls over their shoulders. They had round faces with red cheeks, creamy skin, and their hair was light brown. I was captivated by their appearance and beautiful outfits.

We spent most of our time with the youngest wife, Golnar, who was very young, probably in her late twenties, and who was said to be the favorite. Barzanie was probably in his late sixties. There was no differentiation between which child belonged to which wife; it was fascinating to see them living as one large family with respect for each other. The oldest wife was the one who ran the household and the younger wives were under her supervision.

A Checkerboard of Nights and Days

We had our meals and entertainment in the women's quarters. Sometimes my mother was invited to dinner in the men's quarters, while I stayed in the women's quarters with my siblings and the rest of the female clan.

Mother told us about the rituals of the tribe. When a Kurdish wife was eating, she had to turn her back to her husband because she couldn't be seen chewing in his presence. The rules didn't apply to guests like my mother. She hadn't known this custom existed. Some of our neighbors back in Rezaiyeh were Kurdish, but they were much more modern and didn't follow tribal rituals.

We stayed with the Kurds for ten days, but it seemed much longer because their lifestyle was so foreign to us. When we were ready to leave they presented us with special gifts that filled a large suitcase. They had sent their horsemen to Iraqi Kurdistan, which was under British rule at the time, to bring back special foreign goods like soaps, silk, lovely materials, and British-made towels. We had none of these luxuries in Iran at the time. My mother was hoping to use the materials to make draperies for our reception room.

On our return journey home, when we arrived on horseback at Kermanshah, a city close to our hometown, the border guards searched us to see if we had any foreign goods. We were worried we would have to forfeit all the beautiful gifts given to us, but to our immense surprise they found nothing. When we finally arrived home, mother asked Pooran, who was just ten at the time, "Where are all the gifts that were given to us?"

She replied, "I wrapped the silk and soap in the towels and buried them within in our dirty clothing in the suitcases so the guards wouldn't find them." No one had told her to do that, but my sister was always a sharp, strategic thinker. She grew up to be an amazing and accomplished woman. My father used to call her "Kadbanno," meaning a woman who manages situations very well. She surely lived up to her name that day.

I have many happy memories of my elementary school years. Thanks to Reza Shah and his progressive ideas about education, I was lucky to be attending a modern school. Our teachers were German, British, and French women, mostly wives of Iranian men who had been educated abroad. Reza Shah believed in sending these upper class young men to Europe and the U.S. to study engineering, medicine, and other professions.

Our school had a dance company, a theater group, poetry readings, and a student orchestra, where I played banjo very poorly, unlike Pooran, who was quite talented on the violin. Our German physical education teacher, who was very pretty and dressed in the most modern fashions, had us jumping over hula hoops. Our drama teacher was Armenian. In second grade, I played the role of a young Arab man wearing a long white thawb, the cloak covering my whole body except for my head, feet, and hands, as I recited "I am from Iraq" in Arabic ("Ana min al Iraq").

In elementary and secondary school, I was taught a great deal about ancient Persian history and their advanced civilization. The Persian Empire was established in 550 B.C. and extended as far as Egypt, Macedonia, India, and the Black Sea.

A Checkerboard of Nights and Days

Iran's civilization dates back to 7000 B.C. and it had a great influence on the ancient world. From ancient times Persians were engaged in agriculture, cattle raising, weaving, and making clay. They made tools using stone and copper. Old Persia invented irrigation systems and were the first people to domesticate animals. There was no slave labor in Persia, and male and female laborers were paid equally. Historical documents and ancient art show that women were involved as professionals in all levels of society, including the treasury and financial offices. Over one thousand years ago the great epic poet Ferdowsi, in his famous *The Persian Book of Kings,* spoke about women as powerful and integral members of society. Since ancient times, Persian culture featured women poets, sculptors, painters, musicians, and politicians. My family members carried on Ferdowsi's ideals. Women were considered strong managers and were fully educated.

Pooran was two years ahead of me in school, the oldest child after my brother's death, and during my mother's depression she assumed a tremendous amount of responsibility in the family. She took care of everybody but was more of a mother to my brothers than to me. From early childhood I had always been a very independent minded person. Although extremely quiet, I would do whatever I wanted to do.

Just like my father, Pooran was very kind, generous, and caring. When my mother couldn't sleep after my father's death, she would sit at her bedside and read from Baha'i prayer and history books. Pooran was the most spiritual among all of us.

My paternal grandmother, Kokeb Khanoum, was from a prominent royal family. When my grandfather Yousef decided to take

43

a long trip abroad, my grandmother had asked for a divorce and later remarried a younger man. The family and my father did not approve of her second husband, and as a result she became estranged from us.

My mother had a kind heart and took Kokeb into our home when she became ill with typhoid fever, which was sweeping through Iran. Kokeb was hallucinating due to a high fever and we isolated her in the living room, where we made her a comfortable bed. Our household helpers fed and took care of her. She died ten days later with a picture of her youngest son, Attallah, in her hands. She was crying out for her oldest son, my father: "Haibatullah!" She didn't realize that both of her sons were not with her. My father was away and her youngest son, my uncle, was in Germany, having left in 1937 to study engineering in Hamburg. He was forced to remain there due to World War II and we wouldn't hear from him for another four years. He endured hunger, sickness, and homelessness until he could return to Iran with his German wife. Based on the stories he told us, it was a miracle he survived the war and its massive destruction.

After Kokeb Khanoum died, our household help took the trunk of her belongings to our large storage room. The next day Pooran went to open the trunk to gather my grandmother's important documents. My mother heard a loud scream and ran downstairs at once to find Pooran crying and shaking.

"Grandmother's ghost is talking to me! Her ghost is here! I saw it!"

44

"No, she's gone to heaven. You're okay. Just leave the trunk alone."

Eventually Pooran calmed down, although we never understood what she had seen to cause this hysterical reaction. I thought it was her imagination. She was a very creative and sensitive person.

Six

Reza Shah Pahlavi visited our home city in the late 1930s. He was very proud of Rezaiyeh; it was the first city in Iran to accept his modernization efforts and the population was very supportive of his policies. The Shah had announced the unveiling of all women and encouraged both genders to shun their traditional garb and wear more Western clothes: suits for men, and long skirts and long-sleeved blouses for women. The mullahs vehemently opposed him and declared his policies blasphemy. This schism would play out again under his son's regime many years later and eventually lead to the 1979 Islamic Revolution.

Modernization was accepted more readily in Rezaiyeh than in other parts of Iran because we were close to Turkey, which was already secularized under Ataturk, and near to Russia, which was a modernized country. My father was a progressive thinker who admired the Shah and his policies. My mother had never worn a hijab; as a child she wore a scarf on some occasions.

People prepared for weeks for the Shah's visit. Iranian flags of red, green, and white flew all over. Persian carpets were spread along the sidewalks and hung in front of doors, a common custom for big celebrations. On the day the Shah arrived, people stood along the streets, on roofs, and perched in trees to greet him, singing the new national anthem. My father was one of the dignitaries included in the welcoming committee. Being a patriot and a nationalist, my father strongly believed in the separation of church and state and in individual freedoms.

During the special welcoming ceremony for the Shah, I was the smallest at the end of the line of students who would present flowers to him and his entourage. We stood along a canal under the shade of willow trees with our backs straight, smiling and clapping. Each of us held a bouquet of white and red roses.

I was wearing a new gray uniform with a white collar and cuffs, and could smell the perfume from the bouquet in my hand, tied together with green, red, and white ribbons, the colors of the Iranian flag. Someone from the King's entourage came over, took my flowers, and gave them to someone standing next to the Shah. I didn't have time to be nervous because I never expected my flower bouquet to be picked. My family was very proud that my bouquet had been chosen.

The most important achievement of the Shah's government was freeing women from centuries of oppression. He had made an historic speech at the University of Tehran in 1934, stating that half the Iranian population was going unrecognized and being deprived of its talents and capabilities. He sent government representatives around the country to convince the population that it was time to fight for women's freedom. The campaign was led by foreign-educated men and women activists, who formed an organization for women's rights.

Irandukht Vahidi Fahmy

To reform and secularize the country, the Shah established a centralized government that gave him strong powers. His goal was to limit the influence of the Muslim clergy in government affairs and to separate religion from politics. He created a state department, a department of education, girls' schools, and colleges. He founded the first university in Tehran, one of the biggest and most prestigious schools in the country, which trained researchers and scholars.

The Shah encouraged his wife and daughter to attend official ceremonies in public without wearing the hijab. Over time, women were liberated. They could participate in public life and were more capable of educating themselves and their children. They worked in government offices and studied to become doctors, engineers, and teachers.

The unveiling was the most difficult task for the government. The clergy (Muslim Ulema) vehemently opposed the Shah and considered his declaration blasphemy. Many families throughout the country, especially illiterate and uneducated men, refused to send their wives out in public without the hijab. The king enforced the unveiling by law.

In Rezaiyeh the unveiling was welcomed by the majority of people. I remember my grandmother, grand aunt, and all of their friends were wearing Western clothes by the 1940s. Throughout childhood I never covered my head with a scarf, nor did my mother or female relatives. Only if we were in an area where there was a mosque or bazaar would we wear one; if we didn't, we would have been in real trouble. In college I wore formal western clothing—a suit with stockings and high heels. All the younger generation wore western clothes.

I was still in elementary school when I first understood that Iranian culture was male dominated. When I was in 5th or 6th grade I went to my friend's house and saw how much control her father had over the girls in the family. I realized that my siblings and I had been named by our father with no say from my mother, a traditional part of Iranian culture.

My mother, like my grandmothers, was a strong and independent woman, with a sharp mind and strong will. She had four years of elementary education in a French missionary school in Rezaiyeh, although schooling for girls was forbidden at the time and they were usually educated at home. My mother's father felt strongly that it was important for girls to be educated. Unlike most Iranian women she could read and write, and was very good at handling finances.

My mother was more in control of the house than most women because my father was gone all day long, but I saw how my two uncles dominated their wives; the only thing they were allowed to do was cook and they had no social lives whatsoever. I saw how my younger uncle would buy clothes for his wife because he thought she wasn't capable of doing so herself. He did all the shopping for the same reason; she had no say in the most basic affairs of the house.

Although my parents taught us that men and women were equal, I saw that these ideals weren't being practiced. The country paid lip service to equality, but the culture remained traditional and patriarchal.

Even during the modernization period most families would not allow their daughters to continue education beyond high school. In my family education came first and my mother didn't want to marry away her daughters before they completed their schooling. Most of my female friends were preparing for their arranged marriages. Two of my good female friends insisted that their families send them to Tabriz University. Their parents agreed, as long as they lived in a convent with French nuns so they could be closely supervised. They were already engaged to their second cousins and as soon as they completed their studies they would be married. One of them graduated while the other quit after her first year of college. I knew from quite an early age that my parents would have a major say in who I would marry. Not by arranging my marriage, but by blocking my choice if they didn't approve.

Pooran became engaged to a man from a conservative Muslim family and they wanted her to become Muslim. Her fiancé told her, "Just tell my parents that you're Muslim, but you don't have to practice Islam. You don't have to come to the mosque." Even though my sister had her own reservations about the engagement, it was my mother who laid down the law: "Absolutely not."

Mohammed Reza Shah Pahlavi, who ruled Iran from 1941 until the 1979 upheaval, continued his father's policy of modernization. There was a great deal of improvement culturally and socially, but this was not quite Westernization because the government didn't want to compromise deeply-rooted Iranian culture and tradition. The most social progress I noticed was among Iranian women.

A Checkerboard of Nights and Days

The number of females at the universities increased dramatically. More women were doctors, engineers, scholars, writers, and poets. Much later on, in 1963, Iranian women won the right to vote.

Yet even though the Shah had liberalized the country, women still lagged very far behind. The majority of women were home-makers and not in the work force, except for teachers and nurses. When I attended Tabriz University there were probably six women in the medical school. It was only years later that Iran had more female doctors than most countries in the Middle East. After the revolution they left the country for the U.S., Canada, and Europe.

Unfortunately, the great strides made in women's rights lasted only forty-five years. In 1979 Mohammed Reza Shah was forced to abdicate the throne and leave the country, and the fundamentalist revolution put women back under cover. This was enforced with threat and imprisonments, as the new government required abso-lute obedience to Islamic sharia law. I did not visit the city of my birth after the revolution, but I heard stories from visiting Iranians who left in the 1980s and 1990s. I recently attended a dinner party where I met a highly educated, prominent family that was visiting the U.S. from Iran. This family had two young girls and I was sur-prised to see them dressed in the latest Western fashions that you might see in New York or Los Angeles: short skirts and sleeveless tops, and they wore eye makeup and lipstick. They had iPhones and Skyped with their friends in Iran. They told me they lived two different lives: when they returned to Iran they had to wear their scarves and long coats to school.

The reality of their lives deeply affected me. They spoke of oppression, rage, suffering, anxiety, and fear. They told stories of torture, killings, and disappearances. People were frightened and worried about their families' safety, the state of their country, and the suffering of their people. They told me Iran was afflicted by incivility, corruption, and a ravaged economy. I was heartbroken and saddened for the people who had to live under these oppressive conditions.

It seemed so strange to me that a theocracy ruled the country in the name of God and their religion. What happened to the country of writers and poets like Ferdowsi, Sadi, and Rumi, who preached love and happiness for human beings? In one of his poems, Mevlana Rumi stated: "Faith in God is an inoculation against the diseases of the world, especially loneliness."

The lover visible
And the Beloved invisible—
Who ever saw such a love
In all the world?

When I lived in Iran, the country was progressive, secular, and ethnically diverse. I have been blessed with the opportunity to live in American, a democratic country with personal freedom, dignity, and peace. I have come to realize that the fundamental human need and aspiration is for freedom, open societies, and self-determination. Individual liberty and human rights should be the code of every civilization.

Seven

In the years following my happy elementary school days, I was transformed into a sad and anxious daughter. The repercussions of World War II and the years that followed would bring tragedy and turmoil to my family.

Reza Shah Pahlavi refused to enter the war and declared Iran neutral. Nevertheless, the Soviets invaded Iran from the north and the British invaded from the south. The Soviets wanted a supply route through Iran to receive shipments of food and weapons from the Americans and British to fight Germany. The Allies were unhappy with the King's pro-German policies and asked him to expel German advisors, doctors, and engineers from the country. He refused to do so and was forced to give up the throne in 1941 to his eldest son, Mohammed Reza Pahlavi, who, at just twenty years of age, was very inexperienced in governing the country.

In the winter of 1943, a withdrawal from Iran by the U.S., Britain, and Russia was negotiated; all three countries were to leave within six months' time. President Roosevelt negotiated with Churchill and Stalin, declaring that the war was placing a burden on Iran and that Iranian independence should be respected. Great Britain and America met the deadline, but the Soviet leaders broke the agreement, sent additional troops into the country, and established a puppet government in the north.

In northwest Iran, the leftist and pro-communist Iranian population rebelled against the central government or Iran, as the Soviets encouraged the cessation of Kurdistan and Azerbaijan. My city suddenly became an occupied zone ruled by a foreign culture and communist ideology. Religious books and practices were banned, and we were required to register as members of the communist party. We were forced to stop speaking Farsi, and school instruction was conducted in the Azeri-Turkish language; the books we used came from neighboring Russian Azerbaijan and reflected a communist view of the world. Rezaiyeh was wracked by unrest; we were under siege and stress. An eight-p.m. curfew was imposed, and I vividly remember Russian soldiers patrolling the streets and questioning people. Sometimes we didn't have school for extended periods of time. It was devastating to live under such a regime.

People were afraid for their lives during the Russian invasion. I was old enough to remember my dad standing at the window and crying out, "Oh my goodness, the Russians are bombing us!" We ran to join him and saw a bomb hit our schoolyard just two blocks away. The roar was deafening; our entire house shook and the sky was full of flames.

There were shortages of everything, including food. Luckily, we were an agricultural city and the surrounding farms kept us from going hungry, but there was always a great shortage of sugar, oil, and bread. For us to give up sugary tea was a great hardship. The Russians were taking all of our food supplies.

My mother was so creative in dealing with the sugar short-age. She boiled down grape syrup to make brown sugar cubes. Everyone came by to learn how to do it. She also made dessert from the syrup, such as halava, rice pudding, and some kind of hard candy. My mother tried her best to protect us from the harshness and danger that surrounded us.

Still, life was radically different from what we were used to.

I was aware of what was going on because my dad had talked politics with us from a very young age. By the time I was a teenager, I knew the political systems of a majority of countries in the world. I knew the difference between communism and capitalism, and we knew the Soviet Union wanted to dominate Iran, particularly Azerbaijan, and make it part of their country. It was an economic prize because of its climate, agricultural products, and mining.

My father was very astute and well-informed about international politics because my paternal grandfather was the headmaster of the American College in Rezaiyeh in the 1920s, and had travelled all over the Middle East and Europe. My grandfather journeyed to the U.S. before World War I, which was rather rare for an Iranian at the time. He passed down his cosmopolitan view of the world to my father, who in turn passed it down to us. My father strongly believed in peace and was a humanitarian. He was certain that our lives would eventually improve.

During the occupation, the leftist Russian puppet government was recruiting intellectuals and educated men to join the Communist Party; if they refused, they could be arrested or murdered. Anxiety and panic swept throughout the population. My father decided to leave home and go to Tehran, which was not under leftist rule and where he could work. As a government employee and anti-communist, his life was at risk in Rezaiyeh. He was eventually assigned to a post in Gorgan, a city in northeast Iran where there was no sign of the Russian occupation.

The night he left we gathered around him to say goodbye. When it was my turn, my father gave me a hug that I thought would never end. We were crying but we comforted each other as best as we could.

"Oh, he'll come back," Pooran said. "The occupation won't last forever. Everything will be okay again one of these days, and we'll see our father soon."

One gloomy and chilly night in the fall of 1945, I was in bed with my heavy sweater and warm pants, buried under a woolen blanket in a deep sleep. Due to the curfew, people were not allowed to leave their homes at night, and because of the fear of gunfire all of us slept in the same room. I was awakened by a hard knock on the bedroom window. My frightened mother jumped up from the bed, trembling in fear. Had Russian soldiers come to ask about my father's whereabouts?

When I joined my mother at the window, three Russian soldiers were looking up at us from the street and pointing to their mouths. My mother cracked the window and saw they wanted something to eat. She handed them some bread and cheese left over from our daily meal, and they were thankful for the meager food.

For one year, we had no direct communication with my father. Sometimes he sent us money with someone who was traveling to Azerbaijan. That's the only way we knew he was alive and safe.

A Checkerboard of Nights and Days

We felt so vulnerable. Rezaiyeh was caught up in food short-ages, unrest, and killings, and we didn't have our father around to help shelter us. We were always scared, living day to day in extreme uncertainty. We left our home only for school. Our maid Jayran, a young girl who was Pooran's age, did all the shopping for us. Sometimes there were no goods to be had and the stores were closed. My mother had to be stronger than ever, and we helped her out as much as we could.

When we heard gunfire at night we huddled downstairs in the courtyard, afraid of being shot through our windows. We were always fearful about leaving the house. We routinely heard stories that people were disappearing. It was the most difficult period of my life as a teenager.

But one bright memory I have amid the darkness is of Russian ballet dancers performing in the middle of the street as crowds gathered, and we watched their pirouettes and arabesques from our window. It was so odd to see this wonderful part of Russian culture in the midst of the soldiers' uniforms and submachine guns; they apparently wanted to convince us that our occupiers had a human side.

Aside from the money my father sent home, my mother earned income by selling a wheat plantation that her father had left to her; she also had some inheritance from her parents. The money didn't last long because she had four children to support.

Manoochehr, who was very young at the time, remembers going with my mother to sell a piece of jewelry when we ran out of cash. I recall that my mother gave our beautiful silver samovar tea set to shopkeepers as barter. Years later in San Diego we talked about this, sharing a great deal of remorse that most of our family's treasures were lost during the Soviet occupation.

Every day we waited for our beloved father to return, and we were elated when a telegram arrived, stating that he would be home within a week or ten days. The telegram said he would first stop at my grandfather's house in Tehran to give him a special gift—a lambskin coat handmade by the natives of the region where he worked, and a container of cooking oil.

Ten long, anxious days passed with no sign of my father. I would sit on the windowsill, expecting him to walk down the street any moment. My aunt later told me that my grandfather was out of his mind with worry when my father didn't arrive at his home in Tehran as expected. He finally called the office where my father worked, only to be told that he had left for Tehran two days previously and should have already arrived.

My grandfather sent a relative to look for my father, who returned with shattering news. According to witnesses, my father had stopped at an inn on his way to Tehran. During the night, the witnesses heard sounds of a struggle in his room but didn't bother to get involved. The next morning the innkeeper found my father unconscious on the ground outside the inn with no identification; he had apparently been thrown through the window of his room to the hard ground below.

My grandfather went to search the hospitals in Tehran and the surrounding areas. A young nurse told him that an unidentified patient, apparently unconscious, had been brought to the hospital wearing only his shirt and pants. He was told: "We didn't know who he was, we didn't recognize him, and he passed away in the hospital."

My grandfather was devastated. He received conflicting accounts—some said he died in the hospital, others said that my father was dead on arrival. Either way, he was taken away for burial to an unknown location by someone unknown. The only items he left behind were his slacks, underpants, undershirt, the lambskin coat, and a blanket. My grandfather identified the clothing as my father's.

The innkeeper told my grandfather that Russian "guests" were staying at the inn on the same night as my father. Our suspicion grew that he was killed by communist agents because of his political views. My grandfather went to investigate, travelling by bus to the inn. He was told that there were indeed Russian soldiers staying there, but the motive could also have been burglary because my father's wallet was missing. He could have been killed for his politics, for his money, or both; we will never know the truth.

I was standing next to my mother when she received the news by letter. We were completely overwhelmed. The various stories and rumors were so confusing; we didn't know what to believe and which story to trust. Maybe none of the stories were true. Maybe he was alive and well, and would come home when it was safe, or maybe the Russians had taken him to their country and imprisoned him there; we had heard rumors of that happening to people. It was all so bewildering and shocking.

Irandukht Vahidi Fahmy

I couldn't believe that my father was gone forever. I thought one day he was going to walk back into our courtyard and tell us, "It was a mistake. I am alive. I am with you." Not knowing the location of his grave and not having any of his possessions only compounded our devastation.

For many years I was certain he was still alive. When I went to live in Tehran with my grandfather in the 10th grade, I kept expecting that he would show up at our home every day. Sometimes I would look for him in the faces that passed me as I walked the streets of the city. It was heart wrenching to finally realize it was only a fantasy. He was gone forever.

Many years later I had one of the most important conversations of my life with my paternal Aunt Khojesta in Italy. She had been born when her father was in his late 60's, and we talked about how hard it was for her to have a father who was too old to give her any attention. "I never knew my dad," she told me. "He was in his seventies when I was a child. My dad never talked to me, never hugged me, never let me sit on his lap, never carried on a conversation with me."

Like my aunt, I was unable to experience the fundamental connection so crucial to a happy childhood. Her words touched me deeply, because that is what I lost when my father died—his kindness, caring, and warmth.

Eight

Suddenly, irredeemably, I was a girl without a father. My mother became a widow at the young age of 35, left with four children ages two to fourteen. Her parents were gone and her brothers were not much help, busy with their own families. My maternal grandmother had died while my father was away on assignment. My paternal grandfather was in Tehran a thousand miles away and we didn't know him well. He was very distant from us both emotionally and physically.

My mother fell into the second-deep grief and depression of her life, which only increased my sense of loss and sadness. I survived by burying my feelings, just as I had after Aloosh's death, becoming even more quiet and inward. My identity was gone. In Iranian culture, the family's identity was centered in the father's position in the community; he was the head of the household, he named all the children. Before my father's death we were a respected family in our community with financial security; that status and security vanished almost overnight. Now that he was no longer with us, my mother was worried that Pooran and I wouldn't be able to marry well because we had no wealth. Once we were rich girls; now we were poor.

Irandukht Vahidi Fahmy

We no longer had the same nice clothing as our friends. We had one set of clothes for school and one pair of shoes. Because we didn't have much to offer our guests, we couldn't entertain in our home as we had done before.

The financial strain obligated my mother to give up her inheritance. She had sold the wheat plantation for far less than it was worth. Next went her jewelry, her silver, and her beautiful Persian carpets. I remember this so well: we had a fine carpet that had been part of my mother's dowry when she was a bride. Hung on the wall in our living room, it looked like an exquisite hand-painted scene from nature, depicting birds, vibrant flowers, bees, and butterflies. She gave it to a moneylender with the understanding that he would return it to us once we gave his money back. She was a very proud woman; she always wanted to keep her dignity and standard of living. She kept our long-time maid who had been part of our family since she was nine years old, and tried to keep our lives from changing drastically, holding onto the future that she and my father had once planned.

And yet the taxing circumstances made her a stressed and desperate woman. Her personality changed; she became anxious, emotionally distant, and extremely controlling. She was constantly in a state of panic. Her beautiful brown hair turned gray, her skin color yellowed. Her eyes were glassy and she looked exhausted all the time.

Pooran and I pitched in to help with chores that the servants had once done for us. It was during this time that I began, for the first time, to fear my mother. If for some reason we didn't do the chores the way she wanted, she would scream at us hysterically. I was constantly scared that she would lose her temper with us. Sometimes she became so enraged that her entire body shook. Looking back now, it was clear she was suffering from an anxiety attack, but we lived in a society that didn't know how to name this condition and illness, let alone treat it.

At times I felt like an unwanted child and that I was a burden on her. I knew she loved me; she had been a different mother before my father died. She had been very caring and kind, even though we were left alone much of the time with servants and maids. But now, although we tried so hard to help, she was overwhelmed caring for four children alone. We were grieving ourselves. My heart was bleeding and my tears didn't stop for a very long time.

During the summer after I finished eighth grade, mother decided to take a trip with me to Tehran to discuss our future with my grandfather; she left Pooran, Manoochehr, and Bahman with our maid. We also planned to go to the ministry of health to inquire about my father's annuity, since he had been employed by the central government.

I had never met my paternal grandfather before, although I had heard a lot of stories about his life. He had been a teacher of Persian literature at a very prestigious and well-known American school in Tehran. Most of the kings' and ministers' children were educated there. Then he was transferred to be the headmaster of the American College in Rezaiyeh. He was an Ulema (a "learned man"), well-versed in religious history and literature. In addition to Persian, he spoke four languages fluently: English, French, Arabic, and Turkish. He came from a very respected and devout Muslim family in southern Iran that owned a saffron plantation and many large homes.

Our trip to Tehran was very taxing. We took a small motorboat across Lake Rezaiyeh that was supposed to hold about twenty people but carried many more. When we reached Tabriz there was only one seat left on the overnight bus; I sat on sacks of wheat, barley, and rice piled in the middle of the aisle as the bus climbed torturous mountain roads up steep valleys towards the capital city.

We were exhausted when we arrived at my grandfather's house the next day in the afternoon. He was in his seventies at that time and lived in a modest home with his second wife and daughter. We met him in his large library that also served as a living room and bedroom; he was sitting in his chair with an entire wall of books behind him, regarding us with a stoic face. He didn't get up to welcome us, hug us, or even ask us about our trip: my mother was visibly upset but kept a respectful tone as she spoke to him.

"I want to discuss the future and wellbeing of your grandchildren with you. I also want to go to the ministry of health and find out about my husband's pension."

He responded firmly. "I am not in good financial standing. Don't ask me for help. I am old and retired, living on a very tight budget. If you want to send one or two of your children to live with me, it would be fine. But that's all I can do."

In countries under Islamic law, the parental grandfather was expected to take care of his son's children if the son passed away. Of course, it was very embarrassing for my mother to ask him for help because we never knew him well. He never sent us letters or birthday gifts or visited us for as long as I could remember. My father had visited him occasionally but their relationship was strained. My mother would never send her young children to live with him. Moreover, the ministry of health informed us that my father was not eligible for a pension because of his age at the time of his death. After five days we made the arduous return trip to Rezaiyeh, burdened by disappointment and more grief.

Once again, withdrawal was my defense mechanism, my way of coping. Meanwhile, mother clashed constantly with Pooran. My sister was a very caring and helpful person, but she was the complete opposite of my mother's personality. So I learned to keep quiet amid the turmoil even though I was often extremely upset. I'll never forget overhearing my mother saying one day, "Iran is in her own world. She just doesn't care about what's going on in this family." I did care, very deeply, but I couldn't show it. My mother's words hurt my feelings terribly. I can still remember exactly how I felt.

I completed the ninth grade but I don't remember much about that year. When I wasn't concentrating on my studies, I was a withdrawn dreamer. That difficult time reminds me of a poem by Hafez Shirazi:

> *Sit down be the side of a stream*
> *And in rushing of water*
> *Witness the transience of life*

Although my loving father was no longer with me, I kept him alive in my passion for learning and in my search for knowledge. As Shirazi states in another poem:

> *A heart born of love is immortal,*
> *Never dead in the Book of Life,*
> *So it is written, so it is said.*

Nine

Finally, in March of 1946, Stalin announced the withdrawal of Russian troops from Iran. Iranian central government forces returned to power in Azerbaijan, but the Russians had left behind a large number of subversive agents to assist the Iranian Communist Party. We returned to our pre-occupation lives but found ourselves living in a post-war world where the country was still divided. Three major parties struggled for influence. The Tudeh Party, which was a leftist Communist party that had strong backing on college campuses; the National Front, which consisted of the highly educated elite and was supported by the King and backed by the United States; and the Fedayeen of Islam, which was a fundamentalist Islamic party opposed to the government, the elite, and westernization; it eventually came to power during the 1979 Iranian revolution and remains in power today. The poet Mina Dastgheib wrote:

The government of night
Presses its presence
On the corpse of freedom
In the Brightness of Dawn

In 1947 I was about to start high school in Rezaiyeh, but the school only offered a two-year teacher training institute and I didn't want to become a teacher. At the time my goal was to attend medical school. My mother and I decided that I would go to a college preparatory high school in Tehran. So in August, my mother packed a small suitcase with my most essential belongings and put me on a bus to Tehran to live with my grandfather. Given how our previous visit went I wasn't too keen on the idea, but my desire for a quality education made me suppress my misgivings.

Moving to Tehran, an immense city with a culture far different from Rezaiyeh's, was like moving from a small rural town in America to New York City. I had a difficult time adjusting at my all-girls school. I had a heavy accent from speaking Turkish at home and the girls made fun of me. They were cliquish and more social than how I was brought up. They spoke openly about having rendezvouses with boys, which was strange and taboo for me. I was grateful that we wore school uniforms; at least they couldn't make fun of my clothing.

My grandfather wasn't any kinder than when I visited him with my mother. He was a brilliant man, perhaps even a genius, extremely well read, an author, and fluent in five languages. But he wasn't a people person or a family man, the complete opposite of my outgoing father. He didn't know that I existed and treated his own daughter, my aunt, in the same way.

Even though my grandfather was a difficult person to know, he was the most influential person in our entire extended family, and in my life. He came from a very prominent and wealthy family, but his parents disowned him at the young age of 14 because he accepted the Baha'i faith. He learned to survive, moved often, travelled to Karbala in Iraq, and became a scholar of religions and languages.

More than anything, he passed down to me an appreciation for the power of education to transform one's life. For him, education meant not just formal education but informal education—what you learn from life's experiences. His wisdom in this regard was an important part of my life when I was raising my own children.

When I was living in Tehran, my grandmother would make a special and very healthy breakfast for him—eggs, a milkshake with yogurt, cheese, a piece of bread, and tea. Then he would walk at least 100 laps around his yard, even when he was in his seventies. By being so physically fit he was way ahead of his time.

And he was extremely frugal, even stingy. He did not like to spend money. My mother always had money in the house and didn't bother to hide it. My grandfather kept his money in a big trunk, locked under his bed.

One day I watched from a window to see what he was doing. He would unlock his trunk, take out some cash, and put the trunk back under his bed again. Then he beckoned my grandmother and gave her spending money for the day.

He wouldn't allow us in his room; no one could enter except my grandmother who brought him food. He ate in his room surrounded by his books. He was reading all the time, and lecturing at the Baha'i center in Tehran and at various colleges.

A Checkerboard of Nights and Days

Sometimes I would ask him, "Grandpa, what is this word in English?" He would respond right away with the meaning, but that was the only response I would get from him.

Although he was emotionally distant, I respected him for his intelligence, for his education, and for what he accomplished in his life. He was way ahead of his time by travelling all over Europe and to the U.S., where he stayed for two weeks back in 1915 and met Americans of the Baha'i faith. How many people from his part of the world travelled like that in the early 20th century? Nobody in my town traveled when I was a child. No one travelled in the other families I knew. So I think our whole extended family's love of travelling came from him.

I was so lonely and longing for friendship that I thought of my Assyrian childhood friend, Nellie Sarkazian, who had moved to Tehran when I was in sixth grade. Perhaps I could locate her, so I asked another Assyrian girl in my class if she knew of my friend from her church; she said she did and would pass on a letter to Nellie from me. A day or two later I was called to the principal's office at my school to find my grandmother waiting there. The principal had confiscated my letter because he suspected I was writing to a boy, which was grounds for expulsion.

Although I eventually got in touch with Nellie, I was appalled by the close-minded and strict school administration. My life in Tehran continued to be suffocating. We didn't have any social life. My grandparents stayed home all day long. When my grandmother asked my grandfather for money so she could buy new clothes for me and my aunt, he refused: "Why do they need new clothes?

They already have enough clothes to wear." He didn't believe in having worldly goods.

This was such a strange life, because in Rezaiyeh we had friends and socialized. In order to survive this strict household, I concentrated on my studies. I did all my homework and went to sleep early. My grandfather was so frugal he didn't want us using gas lanterns to study at night because gas was expensive. As such, I woke up at six a.m. every morning to study some more.

I was miserable and missed my mother and siblings. After ninth grade ended, I told my grandfather I was going back home. Luckily for me, Rezaiyeh had opened a college preparatory high school, so I could get the education I desired.

While I was away, my mother had rented our large and handsomely furnished reception room to a couple to supplement her income. It wasn't considered proper to rent a room to strangers in your private home, but my mother needed the money. To help out, I tutored elementary school children. That's how I began to tutor Madame Andranic's nine-year-old son in math, in exchange for her teaching me how to sew.

Pooran had already gone on to the University of Tabriz, where she studied education and languages and had a full-time teaching position. When I graduated from high school I decided to enter the University of Tabriz as well. With both her daughters in Tabriz, mother moved there with Manoochehr and Bahman to keep the family together.

A Checkerboard of Nights and Days

It was heartbreaking for her to leave her beloved ancestral home where her family had lived for generations. She was born, raised, and married in Rezaiyeh; her soul belonged to that land. Yet she was ready to leave behind those memories for her children's wellbeing and future. Her decision reminded me of another poem from the *Rubaiyat* by Omar Khayyám:

> *Listen to the reed, how it tells a tale,*
> *Complaining of a separation,*
> *Saying: "Ever since I was parted from the*
> *Reed bed, my lament has caused man*
> *And woman to moan…"*
>
> *The moving finger writes; having writ,*
> *Moves on: nor all your piety nor wit*
> *Shall lure it back to cancel half a line,*
> *Nor all your tears wash out a word of it.*

Ten

We traveled across Rezaiyeh Lake by boat and arrived in Tabriz, the capital of the state of Azerbaijan and its largest city, with a population of almost half a million.

For centuries, the only way to reach this region was through the traditional migration route of the Silk Road. In more recent times, you could travel to Tabriz by boat, bus, or car, but it was still an extremely taxing trip. You needed a lot of patience, courage, and a tough vehicle to reach your destination.

We experienced a great deal of culture shock in our new home, because Tabriz was a city divided. The area where we lived was modern, progressive, and diverse, but the traditional Tabriz community was predominantly Muslim, extremely conservative, and prejudiced towards newcomers. They did not mix with minority groups—college professors and students, people of the Baha'i or Jewish faith, Armenians, and Assyrians. The Muslim community in Tabriz regarded people of different faiths as immoral. We lived in two different worlds, literally: the eastern part of the city was conservative, while our neighborhood in the northwest was secular. For the first time in my life I experienced a distinct separation between ethnic and religious groups, a true segregation. We were never invited to visit any traditional Muslim families from the east.

Because no one knew what religion I belonged to (if any), I never experienced religious discrimination on the streets of Tabriz, but as a woman I experienced discrimination all the time. To assert their authority, young boys and men would jostle against me as I walked down the street, sometimes nearly pushing me around. I had to wear a scarf when visiting the bazaar; otherwise, I would be spat upon but some of the more conservative men.

It was the women who were always singled out, who were always a potential target. Conservative Muslims believed women should not be seen or heard. Some men wouldn't shake a woman's hand or even make eye contact; they always looked down or to the side when I passed them. It was extremely disconcerting and I never got used to it.

One afternoon, a college friend from a wealthy Muslim family invited me to her home in the old section of the city, to see her gardens. We sat on a bench and her family's maid, a very young girl who wore a long black chador with half her face covered, brought tea. No family member came out to greet me. Whenever friends visited my home in Rezaiyeh, my parents and siblings always greeted them. My friend was too afraid to tell her family that I was of the Baha'i faith. She said to me, "My father is a busy merchant in the bazaar." I understood immediately what she meant: I was a different person who was unacceptable to her parents. It was a strange and disheartening experience, but it taught me first-hand about religious intolerance.

One of my other university friends visited a traditional Muslim home for tea as well. At first, they didn't know she was Baha'i.

Irandukht Vahidi Fahmy

When they found out, they smashed and threw out the tea glass she drank from.

Fortunately, I had a few good friends who weren't so judgmental about my religion. Even so, I never went to the historic Jameh Mosque in Tabriz. Built at the beginning of the Islamization of Iran, its huge entrance door was richly decorated with blue and white domes; above it was written "Allahu Akbar" ("God is Great"). Mostly men went to mosques; the women would pray at home five times a day facing toward Mecca.

Near the mosque was the ancient Tabriz bazaar, the city's original trade center, with thousands of stalls piled high with vibrantly colored cottons, woolen fabrics, leather goods, art, silver, and Tabriz's famous carpets. The merchants and tradesmen would pray in the mosque: morning, noon, and evening. They would return home to their yards and gardens secluded behind walls, and their wives would not be seen.

On the outskirts of the city was a vast park, Shahgoli Park, with a covered pavilion and a large pool in the center, surrounded by beautiful, well-kept gardens called golestan (which means "rose garden"). This was the main recreational center for most families to picnic, walk, dine, and enjoy their weekends. A famous poet, Rumi, who lived in Tabriz for a few years, wrote these lines:

> As the sun moving, clouds behind him run,
> All hearts attend thee, O Tabriz's sun!

Tabriz University, newly constructed, was located on the outskirts of the city, the second largest university in the country after Tehran University. It offered Bachelor's degrees in the sciences, humanities, education, languages, religious studies, philosophy, history, and geography. Students could take classes in any of the colleges and combine subject areas. Attached to the university was a very prestigious medical school. Eventually, when I lived in New York City in the 1960s, I met many medical students who had graduated from Tabriz University and came to the U.S. to complete their medical internships and residencies. I majored in education, psychology, and Persian literature at the university. No longer was I interested in medical school; my plans were to eventually attend graduate school at Tehran University and hopefully study for a Doctorate in Persian Literature.

The majority of students at Tabriz University were male, with just ten percent being female. Girls would never talk to the male students; if we carried on even the simplest conversation it meant that we were immoral and interested in boys. In my major, humanities, there were very few female students; in most of my classes I was one of just three women. We always sat in the front and the boys sat in the back rows. We didn't know who they were or where they came from. It was very awkward.

One of the required courses was Islamic history and literature. The professor, who was a mullah (a religious leader), would look at us three girls and order us to go home: "You don't have to be here! It's getting dark!" He wasn't concerned about our safety; he simply believed that women didn't belong in the university.

One day when I was leaving the university, I saw two women standing at the entrance; they were completely covered in the chador veil and stared at me. I didn't think anything of it. The next day I saw them again and began to wonder. Back in class, a shy young man said to me, "Did you see my mother and my sister?"

"Where?" I asked.

"Oh, they were standing at the university entrance. They would like to meet your mother and ask her for your hand in marriage."

"Thank you, but no," I said. I was somewhat surprised that a conservative Muslim family would entertain marrying outside of the faith.

I had two other Muslim friends in college who weren't conservative and wore western clothes. Sometimes we went to a café for sweets or tea. Even though we were friends, I never visited their homes or met their parents. It was a passing or social friendship, not a deep one.

I attended college from eight a.m. to twelve p.m., went home for lunch from twelve p.m. to two p.m., and taught fourth grade during the afternoon session from two p.m. to six p.m. My sister taught physical education classes in the morning and attended college in the evening. As I did during my year in Tehran, I concentrated on work and my studies. My family's financial situation improved somewhat because my sister and I both were teaching, and my mother was receiving rent from our home in Rezaiyeh. Five years after my father's death, our lives were returning to normal.

A Checkerboard of Nights and Days

My brother Manoochehr was in high school in Tabriz. He took on a great deal of responsibility in helping my younger brother Bahman grow socially and intellectually, making sure he did well in school and taking him along for activities with his friends. Pooran continued to play the second mother role in our family, making most of the decisions concerning my brothers. Even though we were both teaching and going to college, my sister and I helped with chores around the house.

My mother needed our help. She was in a new place and had to find her way, and was especially lost without our maid Jayran. When we left Rezaiyeh, we decided not to take her with us. She was twenty years old, and we thought it was time for her to go to her family's village to be married and have children of her own. She was just a nine-year-old girl when she first came to us from my maternal grandfather's village to be the nanny to two-year-old Bahman. We did miss our maid; she had been a loyal part of our family for nearly a dozen years.

In a way, the discrimination in Tabriz brought our family closer together. We had quite a few Assyrian friends and the landlord of the first house we rented was Armenian, so we felt secure in our own enclave. We also had the support of the Baha'i community, which was crucial because the Muslim majority didn't feel we were truly Iranian.

The Baha'i community in Tabriz was very diverse ethnically, nationally, professionally, and socially. Our members came from different religious backgrounds—Muslims, Jews, and

Irandukht Vahidi Fahmy

Christians—because our faith accepted intermarriage between people of different faiths.

It was inevitable that we would be at odds with conservative Islam. Our religion was a threat to their culture because we believed in the equality of all people, the unity of all religions, and world peace. We were taught that unity within diversity and mutual tolerance were important for the wellbeing of society. The values of the Baha'i faith emphasized the abolition of all prejudices, the independent investigation of truth, the equality of men and women, universal education, and harmony between religion and science. The Muslims didn't share the same values that we had; the Baha'i community was too free and liberal for their taste.

As Baha'u'llah, the founder of the Baha'i faith, writes:

> *Ye are the fruits of*
> *One tree, and the*
> *Leaves of one branch.*
> *Deal ye one with*
> *Another with the*
> *Utmost love and*
> *Harmony, with*
> *Friendliness and*
> *Fellowship.*

Another Baha'i writing states:

> *Beyond all differences of race*
> *Culture, class, or ethnicity,*
> *Regardless of differences in*

A Checkerboard of Nights and Days

customs, opinion, or
temperaments, every individual
Is a member of one gloriously
divers human family. Each
unique individual has a role
To play in carrying toward an
Ever-advancing material and
spiritual civilization

My family became followers of the Baha'i faith because of my paternal grandfather, who became a follower at age 14 through his maternal uncle, one of the first believers in the religion. My mother followed her father's faith and considered herself a Baha'i. One of my uncles never accepted the faith, but another uncle became an active member of the Baha'i community.

Both my grandmothers were non-practicing Muslims. My father was a non-practicing Baha'i and so was my mother while we were living in Rezaiyeh. After my dad passed away, one of my dad's distant Baha'i relatives told my mother that she needed to come back to her faith and practice it. She invited us to participate in Baha'i activities and meetings, and my sister and I started to attend a Baha'i school on Fridays. Through the school I became more knowledgeable about my religion.

I had always felt more spiritual than religious, strongly believing in peace, equality, and unity amid diversity, which is why I accepted the Baha'i faith at the age of 14. Unlike other religions, you don't have to become Baha'i simply because you are born into it. When you're 14 or 15 you can choose your faith, and that's what I decided to do. My religion respected women, and I had been taught from childhood that women had a very important role in society. I remember vividly reading in Baha'i literature that you educate your daughters before your sons, because the daughters will become mothers who will then educate their sons. It was a major turning point for me to believe in this philosophy.

While my sister was in Tabriz she became much more involved in the Baha'i community. There were a large number of young Baha'i students at the university who held spiritual assemblies and regular fireside meetings.

The Baha'i faith originated in Persia in the mid-19th century and spread throughout Iran during its modernization. In less than 200 years it became established in every country in the world, with adherents from virtually every nation, ethnic group, and religion. But in today's Iran, people of the Baha'i faith either have to pretend they are Muslim or deny their faith in order to stay in the country. After the 1979 revolution, the Islamic government destroyed the Baha'i center and killed many followers. In Tabriz, one of our college friends who was the head of the Baha'i assembly was killed by an Iranian security soldier. The majority of Baha'is fled Iran as refugees, emigrating to the U.S., Canada, and Australia. Many also live in Europe; my aunt, for example, lives in Verona, Italy, where she and her family teach the faith. I visited her recently and we reminisced until well past midnight about the old days, our memories of childhood, and the Iran we once knew and loved.

The Islamic hardliners believe the Americans and British created the Baha'i faith as a cover for infiltration and intelligence gathering in Iran. This is a far cry from the modernization period in Iran, when the faith spread throughout the country, and Baha'i centers and schools opened in Tehran and other major cities. Even some of the royal family sent their children to be educated in Baha'i schools because the curricula were the most modern in the country, but that changed after the fundamentalists came to power during the 1979 revolution.

In 1953, when I was in college, Iran elected a socialist prime minister, Mohammad Mosaddegh. The Shah stepped down and decided to leave the country temporarily because of many threats against his life. Mosaddegh, with the full confidence of the Iranian people, and total unfettered power, nationalized a British oil company and took control of all foreign assets. This did not sit well with the United States and the United Kingdom. Thus after several months, a pro-Shah coup was orchestrated by the United States' Central Intelligence Agency, and the British intelligence. In a very swift coup, Mossaddegh was overthrown by the Iranian army and the Shah was returned to power.

Manoochehr was a student at Tehran University's School of Engineering and began classes there in September 1953. The student body was very liberal and there was a backlash against the Shah's coup, leading to a major student uprising against the Iranian government. I vividly remember hearing on the radio that there had been a shooting at the university by the state run security forces and the Shah's elite guard. Three students had been killed and many more wounded, the majority from engineering and sciences.

My family was paralyzed with worry about Manoochehr's safety. We didn't know what to do because we didn't have access to telephones. At that time we communicated through letter writing and by sending telegrams, and it would take up to a week to get a reply. For many days we didn't hear from my brother and none of us had a good night's sleep. Finally, after a week, we heard from him. Manoochehr told us that he was hiding behind a tree when he watched one of his best friends get shot by the Shah's secret police, a horror he would never forget.

Eleven

After I received the news in the summer of 1956 that I had received a royal scholarship to study abroad, I moved to Tehran. I waited all of September and most of October to hear official word that I had been admitted for study to the United States. In the meantime, I was assigned to teach math in a girls' public high school for two months. Not having a degree in math, this required a bit of preparation on my part. The young women were well-behaved and there were no discipline problems. They were happy to have me as their teacher because I was young and looked young.

With Manoochehr and I both living in Tehran, my mother and Bahman moved there as well. A Jewish Baha'i woman rented us the second floor of her home. Now we were all together again under one roof, with the exception of Pooran, who was married, living in Tabriz, and teaching at the high school. Her husband Vali was working for the Iranian Central Bank (or "Bankeh Melee") and they were happily expecting their first child.

Since we continued to receive no official news about our scholarships, a group of us would go to the ministry of higher education and sit on the steps, arriving at 9 a.m. and leaving at noon. Our only way to penetrate the bureaucracy was to keep showing up day after day, week after week, to sit on the steps and wait for news. Time was swiftly passing by, and a lot of paperwork and finances would have to be completed for our admission to American and European universities.

Finally, a young man from the ministry named Dariush was assigned to our group. He would meet with us on the steps and excitedly say, "Please! Have patience, we will do our work! We have to get your passports and make sure you're admitted to the universities. It's a very long process. Insha'Allah."

"But when?" we would ask. "We've received no information!"

"Sabre." Patience.

Part of me remained convinced that the scholarships weren't ever real to begin with. We had no dates for when we would leave the country. Every day there was a different excuse. I thought it was just another attempt by the Shah to create positive publicity for his regime; the government was too disorganized and inefficient to set aside a budget to pay for scholarships. I went and sat on the steps for a month and half, until I finally gave up. The other students continued to show up every day waiting for news.

Finally, in November, Dariush told us, "You are invited by the Shah Reza Pahlavi, the King, to the Golestan Palace in Tehran for a reception on Friday afternoon."

On that afternoon in November 1956, four young women and sixteen young men climbed the steps of Golestan Palace (meaning "rose garden"), located on the far end of famous Ferdowsi Street in the heart of the capital city. In front of the palace was a majestic and extraordinary piece called the Takhat-e Maarmar ("the marble throne"), a divan inlaid with colorful stones and decorated with chimaera. The palace's architecture and design was so incredible that I couldn't take my eyes off it.

We were ushered into the entrance hall by the assistant minister of education and our guide. The hall was entirely covered with metalwork that provided light by reflecting the sun, a design very common in ancient Persian mosques, museums, and palaces. At the far end of the monumental royal hall we noticed an eye-catching item of furniture—a peacock throne. It was a square divan with golden legs and thousands of precious stones inlaid into its surface, forming flowers, leaves, and birds. It had been a gift from King Fath Ali Shah to his beautiful and favorite wife, Tavouse Khanoam ("lady of the peacock").

We entered a large reception room furnished with a magnificent 17th century wall-to-wall carpet, the most beautiful Persian carpet I had ever seen in my life, which depicted in its pattern the palace gardens. The walls were lined with pictures of former Persian kings and queens. I was more engrossed in the beauties of the reception room than by the prospect of seeing the Shah.

We were lined up against a wall, the four women in the middle, the men flanking us. I was wearing a gray, long-sleeved, handmade sweater, a mid-length black skirt, stockings, and black high heels. We remained standing as palace butlers dressed in French-style black suits with white shirts, cravats, and gloves served us delicious almond cookies and tea in gold-embossed glasses.

Irandukht Vahidi Fahmy

After a wait of about a half hour, two palace staff opened a large door and a loud voice proclaimed, "Here is the King of Kings."

The Shah walked in, dressed in a dark suit, white shirt and black tie. He started at the beginning of the line, shook our hands, and asked each of us, "Where are you going, and what are you studying?"

When it was my turn he asked, "What is your interest?"

I replied in Farsi, "*Tali Meh Tar Biat.*" ("Education.")

He questioned me in French, "*Pedagogie?*"

"*Baleh,*" I said. ("Yes.")

The king replied, "*Khosh Halem.*" ("I am happy.")

He was very personable and friendly as he continued down the line. He told us he hoped we would return to educate future generations of Iranians. Then he said, "*Safar Bekhar.*" ("A good journey.")

We left the palace to visit its breathtaking gardens, filled with rose bushes and striking plane trees that provided shade, coolness, and silence. This scenery represented Persia perfectly, as poets and writers have called it "The Land of Roses and Nightingales." A group of journalists and photographers surrounded us. The next day our photographs were in the national newspaper all over the country. My friends and family were so proud. My mother was a woman of little words, but I could tell she was very pleased and happy.

A Checkerboard of Nights and Days

Finally, at the beginning of January 1957, we received our passports, visas, and our monthly allowances. The time had come for us to leave the country and head to the United States of America.! We would fly by Air France from Tehran to Paris, then on to New York. All of us would attend the English Language Institute at the University of Michigan to improve our English efficiency before enrolling at the universities of our choice. Later in the month, my family and friends gathered around me at the Tehran Airport to wish me a good voyage.

The stars had aligned to alter the course of my life, because as it turns out, that was the first and only year that the Shah of Iran offered royal scholarships.

Many years later, after my mother died an unhappy woman in Iran, I received a box of her belongings from my brother. When I opened it, I found the photo taken of me at the Shah's reception, shaking the king's hand. In her pride, my mother had saved the photo for decades; when I showed it to my daughter Roya, the both of us burst into tears.

Part Two

With them the seed of Wisdom did I sow,
And with my own hand labour'd it to grow:
And this was all the Harvest that I reap'd—
"I came like Water, and like wind I go"

OMAR KHAYYÁM

Twelve

We flew from Tehran to Paris, where we had a one-night layover. I was staring at the City of Lights from the window of my hotel room, fascinated with the view of the Eiffel Tower, when I suddenly heard screaming. One of young women I was travelling with went into the hotel bathroom to take a bath and didn't know how to turn on the faucet. She finally figured it out, but didn't know how to turn it off. We heard her yelling: "Please, help me! I don't know how to turn off the bathtub! It's overflowing!" That was an amusing highlight of our one night in Paris.

The next morning we flew from Paris to New York City. Two pleasant young men from the Iranian consulate in New York greeted us at the airport. They arranged for us to stay in a New York City hotel for three days and two nights before flying on to Ann Arbor, Michigan to attend the English Language Institute at the University of Michigan, where we would improve our spoken and written English before attending our host universities in the fall.

During our two days in New York we took a brief walking tour of the city. Compared with Tehran and its maddening traffic patterns, where cars would often drive on sidewalks in front of pedestrians, it didn't seem that crowded. New York drivers stopped at red lights and moved at green ones. For the first time I saw skyscrapers, and the flashing lights on billboards amazed me.

One vivid memory I have is of a small store packed with watches, run by a couple of young Indian salesmen. They had a big "60% off" sign in the window. Such a sign was completely foreign to us. In Iran there were no fixed prices on goods and salespeople bargained with their customers. After ten to fifteen minutes of haggling back and forth, the salesmen and buyers settled on a mutually agreeable price.

We visited the Empire State Building and the Statue of Liberty. I had seen pictures of "Lady Liberty", but meeting her in person with the torch held so high in her hand took my breath away. It was an extremely moving experience.

The next day, we flew to the University of Michigan in Ann Arbor. The students were on winter semester break and the campus was deserted. We were assigned to campus housing and there was nothing much to do but wait.

The cafeteria and food services were closed, so we went shopping for food in a small corner grocery store. We bought some bread, cheese, and fresh fruits. The bread was soft and sweet, the cheese was very hard, and the fruits didn't taste luscious and ripe as they did in Iran. Later on, an entrepreneurial student at the University of Michigan started to make Persian thin bread (lavash) in his kitchen and sold it to Iranian, Afghani, and Iraqi exchange students. Eventually he opened a successful bakery in Ann Arbor, Michigan.

A Checkerboard of Nights and Days

I shared a dorm room with two female nursing students from Puerto Rico. One named Olga and the other Maria. They spoke Spanish with each other and English with me. I needed their help in adjusting to the windy and cold climate of Michigan. My clothing was not appropriate for that cold weather and was very different from the American students' clothing. In Iran, I wore a two-piece suit with stockings and high heels, which was too formal for campus life. I had to wait for my monthly allowance from Iran to purchase more casual clothing, like long-sleeved shirts, long skirts, and saddle shoes.

We had orientation classes from 9 a.m. to 1:00 p.m. daily. These classes included the history, culture, and geography of the United States. It was the best orientation to the U.S. we could possibly have had. We studied alongside students from the Middle East, South America, Africa, and Asia, and also learned about their cultures and countries.

I had some knowledge and understanding of U.S. culture because I had studied American history and geography in depth while in high school and college. When I was at the University of Tabriz, Pooran, a language major, had spent some time in the Iranian-American Language Institute. I had the opportunity to meet the U.S. Consul General in Iran, and was invited with a group of college students to attend a cultural exchange session to discuss the American way of life. My grandfather had visited the U.S. in 1915 to teach the Baha'i faith and visit the Baha'i community. He was very impressed with the country's freedom of religion and morality, and the hard work of the American people. But I was the first person in my family to live in the U.S. for an extended period of time.

Irandukht Vahidi Fahmy

Aside from the cultural orientation, the main reason we were at the Institute was to take English as a Second Language (ESL) classes to improve our English before starting our university study in the fall. This was a big challenge for me. I could read and write English, but I couldn't speak it or understand it very well. In classes I couldn't concentrate for more than twenty minutes listening to English. I was extremely frustrated and felt helpless.

In the classroom, I realized anew how different our Persian language was from English. Persian is read and written from right to left, and the grammar is completely different. In English the noun comes first and the verb comes second; it's the reverse in Persian. We don't have gender pronouns; everything is "it." We pronounce "the" as "dee." We don't have the letter "w"; we pronounce it as "v." I found English spelling and pronunciation extremely difficult to master. All of the Iranian students spoke with very thick accents and even today I still have problems with correct pronunciation of English language words.

As part of our orientation we visited Washington D.C., New York City, and Niagara Falls. When we visited the White House, I was amazed by its simplicity compared with the ornate palaces of the kings in Iran. It impressed me that special ceremonies and lavish displays were not outwardly important in the U.S. We also visited the United States Capitol, where I learned for the first time about the three branches of government: executive, legislative, and judicial. I saw the National Mall and the Lincoln and Jefferson Memorials. I was astonished by how huge and impressive everything was. I had seen pictures of these monuments, but seeing them in person took my breath away. We left Washington, D.C. after three days with the understanding that the rule of law and citizens' rights were paramount in the U.S. Little did I know that one day, my youngest daughter Randa would establish her career in law and politics in Washington, D.C., eventually making it her home.

Many international students coming to this country have told me that they experienced quite a bit of suffering when they first arrived. The first six months of adjusting to a new country and culture are very difficult, and that was the case with me. Even though I was emotionally and psychologically ready to be in the U.S. and was enjoying my orientation and classes, I felt lonely and isolated. I missed my friends and family, and the comforts of my home. I had lived for years with my mother and siblings, ate with them, socialized with them, and traveled with them. It was an enormous change to be separated.

At the same time, I was lucky. I came to the U.S. under ideal circumstances, not as an immigrant or refugee, but as a student who was welcomed with open arms and treated very well. The faculty and neighbors from the surrounding community at the University of Michigan invited us to their homes for special holidays, lunch, and dinner.

I remember vividly when a faculty member's wife invited my friend Parvin and me for Sunday brunch. I didn't have the slightest idea what that was. In Iran we had three meals: breakfast, a big meal at lunch time, and a light supper.

I asked my roommate, "What is brunch?"

"You will have your breakfast and lunch together at 10:30 in the morning."

I said, "How can I go hungry until 10:30?!"

"You can have some pastry and coffee before then," she told me.

"I don't like coffee. I never drank coffee! I drink tea."

"Okay," she said, "have you ever had a biscuit?"

"Yes."

"Wonderful. That works."

Since then, brunch has become my favorite meal and I prepare it every Sunday for my family.

Cultural differences around food presented problems for more than one student. One of my American friends told me she had invited a Nigerian student for dinner. He was a diplomat and an extremely polite gentleman.

"I wanted to treat him to the best American dishes," she told me, "so I made roast pork, potatoes, and gravy. We started having a conversation, and I asked him if there was anything special he didn't eat. And he said, 'I eat everything except pork.' I didn't know what to do! I went to my freezer, took out a TV dinner, put it in the oven, and served the chicken and vegetables for dinner. I told him, 'I hope you liked it!' And he said, 'From now on, I'm going to ask for TV dinners when I eat in America!'"

In addition to the support of faculty and students, I had the support of the Baha'i community in Ann Arbor. We got together and socialized and talked about our faith. It alleviated some of my homesickness.

What impressed me the most about the U.S. was the way people lived. They had the freedom to go wherever they wanted and do whatever they wanted to do. But I couldn't get used to how male and female students interacted on campus. They were lying on the grass next to each other in front of the library. Why were they doing that? The social life, especially among young people, was a difficult adjustment for me.

It was especially difficult to relate to young men since I had been brought up not to associate with boys or young men who were not family members. Older professors were no problem because they were like a brother or an uncle, but I couldn't relate to the younger male professors. As was the case back in Iran, I could relate much better to women, and that's where I found my support.

I had developed better skills in English by time we finished our studies in the English Language Institute in May 1957, and in June, I registered for the summer session at Eastern Michigan University to begin my M.A. in educational administration.

In the Spring of 1957, we Iranian students at the University of Michigan decided to get together and celebrate Nowruz, the Iranian New Year. It is traditionally celebrated when the first flowers appear through the snow, at the time of the vernal equinox. All over Iran, even in the driest and coldest parts of the country, bulbs, flowers, and trees come alive. The Persian New Year is the most cherished of festivals, rooted in the tradition of the

Irandukht Vahidi Fahmy

Zoroastrian faith that worshipped nature, earth, air, fire, and water, and that believed in the opposite elements of light and dark, the angel and the devil. For Zoroastrians, the lord and god of life is Ahura Masda, the great philosopher, the spiritual embodiment of the truth and righteousness that created all that is good. They also believe in a hostile spirit known as the god Ahriman, who created all that is evil and darkness.

Now the New Year reviving old Desires,
The thoughtful Soul to Solitude retires,
Where the White Hand of Moses on the Bough
Puts out, and Jesus from the Ground suspires.

THE RUBAIYAT, OMAR KHAYYÁM

Nowruz is a secular holiday in Iran, celebrated for two weeks and full of earthy symbolism. A traditional tablecloth (called a sofreh) is spread on the floor or on the table. The sofreh is then arranged with seven items starting with the letter S, representing wishes for the coming year. Samanu is a sweet pudding made from wheat germ and is an offering. Sekkeh means gold coins, which symbolize property. Senjed is dried olester fruit, which symbolizes love. Serkeh is vinegar, which symbolizes age and patience. Sib is an apple, which symbolizes health and beauty. Sumac means sunrise, and Sonbal means flowers. There are extra items symbolizing the spring: Sabzeh (sprouted wheat buds) and mahi (live fish in a bowl). There is a belief that if the fish swim on their sides in the bowl, the new year will be a good one.

Schools and government offices are closed during the holiday, and bazaars and stores are decorated with woven rugs and flowers.

A Checkerboard of Nights and Days

Children receive gifts from their parents after first visiting the family elders. Nowruz meals consist of white fish and rice with spinach, parsley, and green onion. Many Iranian families sow cress or wheat seeds in terracotta pots as a symbol of nature's renewal. The final day of Nowruz, March 13th, is called Sizdah be-dar, the Festival of Nature, a special day for outings and picnicking. People leave their homes to enjoy the outdoors and mark the day by planting greens in their yards, praying for a good harvest, and hoping for tranquility in the coming year.

When I eventually settled in Pennsylvania with my own family, I would buy unbleached wheat seeds, called wheat buds, every year at the Philadelphia Flower Show, and plant them in fourteen small pots. After three weeks of growth, the pots would sprout wheat greens six inches high, like lush, green grass. I then would give them to all my friends as a Nowruz gift.

In the spring of 1958 Michigan Governor Mennen Williams and his wife invited all the Iranian students in the state to the governor's mansion in Lansing for a Nowruz celebration. We were served tea and Iranian sweets, and the governor gave each of us a citation with his seal on it that said, "Happy Nowruz." We were so thrilled by his thoughtfulness and kindness.

In March 1959, when I was at Teachers College at Columbia University, a group of us were invited to the Iranian Embassy in Washington, D.C., for a huge Nowruz celebration. The Iranian Ambassador to the U.S. was His Excellency Ardeshir Zahedi, the son-in-law of the Shah. The embassy was famous for its lavish and extravagant parties, featuring singers, dancers, and fabulous Iranian food. It was the best Nowruz celebration I have attended in my life. Whenever I meet some of the old diplomats who served in Washington, D.C. during those years, they vividly remember the wonderful parties at the Iranian Embassy. The bilateral relationship between Iran and the U.S. was very strong in the late 1950s, and throughout the 60s and 70s. That is one of the main reasons why there were so many Iranian exchange students at American universities during that period.

The American students and people I encountered were very kind and respectful to me. They were curious, asked questions, and wanted to learn about my country. Most Americans had heard of Persian rugs and Persian cats but knew nothing more about Iran. Some people I encountered had never even heard of the country. Academics knew Iran was a Middle Eastern country, yet they didn't know Iranians weren't Arabs. We spoke Farsi, not Arabic. I had to tell them that Iranians were originally Aryans who came from Middle Europe and East Asia and settled between the Persian Gulf and Caspian Sea.

Americans had a lot of trouble with my name. They couldn't pronounce Irandukht.

"Call me Iran," I'd say.

"I-ran?"

"No. 'I' pronounced like 'e'."

"Oh, Iran, like the country."

A Checkerboard of Nights and Days

I would tell them that a person's name in Persian culture reflected one's culture, class, beliefs, and ethnicity. Educated families mostly named their children after ancient Persian kings, queens, flowers, heroes, and legends, like the poets Sadi or Ferdowsi. Other common names come from the kings, such as Cyrus the Great or Darius. My brothers' names, Bahman and Manoochehr, are both old Persian names. The religious people usually named their children after the prophet Mohammad's relatives, like Fatima, his wife, or Ali and Hussein, his grandsons.

During the summer of 1957, as I took graduate courses in educational psychology and art history at Eastern Michigan University, I was assigned to a faculty advisor who was extremely understanding of my language limits. The content of the courses was not difficult for me, but it was very challenging to write term papers and conduct research in English. I spent an average of six hours a day in the library. Starting in the fall of 1957 and continuing through the summer of 1958, I took courses toward an M.A. in educational administration, completing that degree in July 1958.

In May 1958, I received confirmation that I had been admitted to Teachers College at Columbia University in New York City beginning in the Fall of 1958, to complete my doctorate in education. With a great deal of regret, I had to leave Michigan behind with all the kindness, hospitality, and friendship that I received from the faculty, students, and citizens of Michigan, all of whom I was proud to call my friends.

Thirteen

In Michigan, I had been befriended by a young family, the Meyers, who had two little girls, ages six and eight. They hosted me often in their home for dinners, and we became very close friends, staying in touch even after I left Michigan. When I was preparing to leave Michigan for New York City in August 1958, Mrs. Meyers helped me purchase my bus ticket.

The trip was an adventure. It was supposed to take nine hours but took thirteen because there were so many stops along the way. I left Ann Arbor at 9 p.m. and didn't get to New York City until 10 a.m. the next day.

I took a taxi to the International House, located between W. 122nd St. and Riverside Drive, adjoining the Columbia University campus. There I received unexpected news.

The receptionist informed me, "I'm sorry, we received your letter to reserve a room but we were already filled." I had never received their letter informing me of this.

I didn't know what to do; I was exhausted and didn't know one soul in New York. When I asked the receptionist for help, she told me there were rooms available in the neighborhood and handed me a list that I could call. I left my suitcase with her, went to the public pay phone, and called five places on the list. All the rooms were taken. Then I found an advertisement on a bulletin board for a room for rent with an address, but no telephone number. I went back to the receptionist and asked her where the address was.

"It isn't far," she said. "Walk three blocks to 125th Street. There's an apartment building there called the Poinciana." She pointed me the way and off I went.

I was trembling as I walked along with my suitcase, looking for the address. In Michigan they told me that New York City wasn't safe and that Columbia University was located in a very dangerous neighborhood.

I finally found the apartment, knocked, and a sweet lady who looked to be in her seventies opened the door. I asked her if she had a room for rent.

"I'm alone, living by myself," Mrs. Goldstein said. "I need company and plan to rent my bedroom. If you don't mind having my bedroom and sharing the kitchen, I would be glad to have you. I'll sleep on the couch."

I asked her how much the room was. She told me $7 a week. In New York City? I was thrilled but told her I would sleep on the couch.

"No, no," she insisted, "you take my bedroom, I will sleep on the couch. You can share my kitchen and cook whenever you want to cook."

Irandukht Vahidi Fahmy

I stayed with Mrs. Goldstein for six months and will never forget her kindness and caring. One day she asked me how my day went. I told her that I was shopping and found a beautiful winter coat that I wanted to buy for the holidays, but I had to wait for my monthly stipend check from the Iranian government to purchase it. I remember the coat was $39, expensive for that time.

"Here's the money," she said. "Please go and buy the coat, and you'll pay me later when you get your money." Sometimes she would insist that I share the dinner she had made. I felt so much at home with her, as if she was a second mother. Meeting people like Mrs. Goldstein, how could I not love the U.S.?

I lived with Mrs. Goldstein for my first semester at Teachers College. Then a room opened at the International House, and I moved there in January 1959. I was a full-time student, taking four graduate courses each semester. My major was education, and it kept me quite busy.

There was so much I loved about the U.S., yet my first year in the country continued to be difficult. Even after the intensive language instruction in Ann Arbor, I still couldn't communicate well in English. The loneliness at times was unbearable as I didn't have any close friends in New York City. In my courses, I couldn't listen to lectures in English for more than 15 minutes before I lost concentration and couldn't absorb any more. It took me hours to read textbooks and finish even the easier term papers. It was so hard to read from left to right! If I had been happier with my life in Iran, I would have returned to my country. I persevered because I knew that returning was not an option.

A Checkerboard of Nights and Days

In February 1959, my mother wrote me that my youngest brother, Bahman, had been admitted to the University of Michigan. He flew to London and traveled by boat to New York City. I was elated to see him after two years. He brought me an exquisite silk rug that I later gave to my son Raef as a wedding present. My mother had sent along a gold Swiss watch for me as a gift, but Bahman was very upset when border agents took it away at customs. He told me, "I wish I hid it, but it was right here in my shirt pocket." Too bad he hadn't been as clever as Pooran, who saved our gifts at the border after we visited the Kurdish tribe twenty years earlier.

Once again, Mrs. Goldstein extended her kindness and welcomed Bahman by providing him with a bedroom. He stayed with her for two days and then I bought him his bus ticket and sent him to Ann Arbor, Michigan to begin his studies. I also called my old friend Mrs. Meyers to make sure she welcomed him to Michigan.

Four days later I was walking home from classes and noticed my brother sitting in a café near campus. Did he have a twin? Was I mistaken? Wasn't Bahman already in Michigan?

I walked up to him and said, "What happened!? Why did you come back!?"

"I didn't pass my English language efficiency exam."

He told me he didn't find his name listed with those who passed. I couldn't believe it because his English was very good. He was back in New York City to enroll in a three-month course in English, and I told him he could stay with Mrs. Goldstein again.

Shortly thereafter, I received a call from my old friend Mrs. Meyers asking where my brother was. When I explained the situation, she said, "No, he passed! I saw his name on the second posting! Tell him to come back right away." The next day I put him on a bus again back to Ann Arbor.

Bahman decided to study engineering at the University of Michigan. We stayed in touch mostly by letters; telephones weren't that accessible in the late 1950s. During his first semester, he wrote me that the freshman math classes were covering the same material he had learned in his sophomore and junior years at his Iranian high school. The math professor would put a formula on the board and Bahman would immediately solve the problem. The professor said, "There's a genius in our class who knows all the answers!" Bahman received straight A's his first semester.

In the summer of 1959 he visited me in New York City, and then went on to work at a resort area in the Finger Lakes region of New York, waiting tables during the day and playing the accordion at night. The old ladies enjoyed his music and gave him $10 tips. Between the tips and his salary, Bahman made a nice sum of money by the end of the summer.

When he returned to Michigan for his sophomore year, he met a pretty young lady named Kathy who was a student at Eastern Michigan University in Ypsilanti. By his sophomore year they were married although none of the family knew about it. He was just 21 and my mother would certainly not have approved.

I found out the news during Christmas break. I called him to say I wanted to visit Michigan, but he stopped me short.

"What's the matter?" I asked.

"I'm married and have a child, a baby boy."

"Congratulations. Such wonderful news. Why didn't you tell me?"

Apparently, their son was born while they were still dating, so Bahman chose to marry Kathy. It would have been a big scandal and caused a great deal of shame in our family if my mother had found out. So I kept this news to myself. Eventually, Pooran handled the situation and broke the news to my mother. In Pooran's caring and kind way, she managed to calm my mother down.

Bahman graduated from the University of Michigan with a Bachelor's degree in mechanical engineering. He went on to get his Master's degree at the University of California in San Diego, and then completed his Ph.D. in computer engineering. He and Kathy eventually had two more boys for a total of three sons: two are lawyers and the other owns a construction company in Southern California. Bahman, my baby brother, has three grandchildren. Along the way, he and Kathy eventually divorced, and he now lives in Northern California with his second wife, a young Indonesian woman named Uni.

During his illustrious career, he worked for the U.S. Agency for International Development and traveled all over the world setting up computer systems for universities. He lived in Indonesia for a year to train university professors in computer science, which is where he met his second wife.

In February 1959, I was visiting my close Turkish friend Afratt in her dormitory room at the International House. The telephone rang in the hallway, and I picked it up. It was another student from Columbia's Teachers College named Mahmoud Fahmy, who I had seen around campus and knew from some of my classes. He asked me if Afratt's roommate was in.

I told him that she had left for Florida, but Afratt was still in town. But for some reason, Mahmoud wanted to talk to me. He asked me if I would like to go with him to a celebration of the United Arab Republic and I quickly accepted. It was a big, lavish party in downtown New York with Arabic music, belly dancers, and plenty of Middle Eastern food, in honor of the political union between Egypt and Syria. Major dignitaries from throughout the Arab world were there. Mahmoud had been invited because he was the Vice President of the Arab Students Organization at Columbia University. I was very impressed with him; everyone seemed to recognize him and he was friendly with all. After that we became good friends. We spent our time studying in the library, socializing with mutual friends, and going out for New York pizza.

From the start, I liked Mahmoud as a friend. He was very polite, generous, caring, and kind. As international students, we had common interests and understood each other's struggles. Mahmoud was awarded a government scholarship to Columbia University from his native country of Egypt in 1958. He arrived in New York City on February 4, 1958 during a snowstorm. He didn't even have an overcoat, but was delighted to see snow for the first time. The very next day he rushed out and bought a warm woolen coat, hat and gloves.

L iving in the International House was an unforgettable experience as I met students from all over the world—Nigeria, India, and the Middle East. Through our discussions, I learned so much about their countries and cultures. By now I was much less isolated and had three close friends from Iran. One eventually became a well-known artist and painter, Iran Darroudi. At the time I met her, she was a student at the Art Institute of New York. After she completed her studies, she married an Iranian and they returned to Iran in the 1960s. They were extremely happy; he worked for Iranian TV, and she was painting and having art exhibitions all over Iran and Europe. I visited her in 1968 when I went to Iran, and so thrilled to reconnect with her.

I lost touch with her after the Iranian revolution in 1979, and didn't know if she still lived there, but I always thought of her. I knew that her family had a home in France, so in 1986 when I was visiting Paris, I decided to try and locate her. The hotel's receptionist where I was staying was from Iran, and I asked him if he knew of my friend Iran Darroudi. He didn't, but was kind enough to give me an address for a great Iranian restaurant in Paris. While dining there, I decided to continue my search for my good friend and asked the waitress, "Do you know Iran Darroudi?"

"Of course! She eats lunch here and she's good friends with the manager."

I couldn't believe it. I asked if they could give me her phone number. They didn't have it but gave me her address. She lived two blocks from the restaurant, but they didn't have the apartment number.

I walked there and rang the bell. The doorman told us she lived on the second floor. There were four apartments but I didn't know which one was hers, so I knocked on the first door we came to.

Someone asked, "Who's that?"

I immediately recognized Iran's voice and told her to open the door. When she did, she was in shock. She looked aged and tired, and told me the story of losing everything before they escaped the Iranian revolution in 1979. The incoming Iranian regime confiscated all of her belongings and bank accounts, and fired her from her job. It was an unbelievable coincidence that I finally found her and we had such a wonderful visit. Later she came to the U.S. and got in touch with me, and we had another great visit where we reminisced about our great times in New York City.

In the summer of 1959, I got a job as a counselor at a Girl Scout sleepaway camp in Long Island, New York. This was another novel learning experience, my first encounter with American teenagers. They came from well-to-do families and were simply spoiled; they brought so many belongings to camp that we had to find a special room to store everything. I was responsible for six of the girls, and we all slept together in a small cottage. Sometimes they would wake up in the middle of the night and scream, "We're afraid of animals! There are animals outside!" Then they would run out the cottage door into the dark night. I was so frightened and did not know what to do. Another counselor told me, "Don't pay attention to them, they'll come back." And they did. The experience was very helpful in my acculturation to the lives of American teens.

A Checkerboard of Nights and Days

In September 1959, Mahmoud proposed to me. I was happy and excited, yet at the same time concerned about the future.

I was 26 years old, mature enough to think very carefully about marriage. It had been a year since I met him and I knew him very well. The only problem I saw was that he was a passionate person, not a logical one as I was. I make decisions with logic, not emotion, and I thought we would always clash. At the same time, Mahmoud was a wonderful person with a good future and we had a lot in common. He had a very solid family background and was well-educated. I would never marry someone who wasn't educated—that was out of the question.

Also, like me, he had grown up in a diverse, secular environment. His mother and father, who were born in Alexandria, Egypt, were very spiritual and pious Sunni Muslims but were not fanatics or extremists. Among his family, friends, and neighbors were Armenians, Jews, and Copts. Yet we still wondered if the marriage would work for us. We were from different countries, spoke different languages, and belonged to different faiths.

We sat down and talked a lot about our commonalities and differences, and our expectations of each other. I knew that Mahmoud would be a wonderful husband and father.

I said yes to his proposal, with the condition that I had to have my mother's permission; in the Baha'i faith you cannot marry without it. I wrote to my mother that Mahmoud was a graduate student from Egypt and a very good person. Mahmoud wrote to his father and received a wonderful letter granting him permission, along with the question: "Where are you going to live? Iran, Egypt, or America?" Of that we weren't yet sure.

Three months went by with no word from my mother. Finally, I told Pooran that I was going to marry Mahmoud whether she accepted it or not, even if I couldn't have a Baha'i ceremony. So my sister, God bless her, went to my mother and said, "Listen, Iran is old enough to make her own decisions. Whether you agree or don't agree, she's going to get married." My sister convinced her, and after four months my mother sent her permission. Pooran wrote the letter and my mother signed it.

I found out later on that my mother was very upset for several reasons. First, she didn't want me to marry in the U.S. She was expecting me to return to Iran and get married there. Marriage in Iranian culture is a matter of logic, not romance. If both families like each other, and their social, educational, and financial statuses match, their children get married. In Iranian culture people strongly believe they are marrying the family, not the person. This logic might appear odd to the Western world, but the success rate for such marriages is probably better than falling in love and marrying someone of a different background. At any rate, I was depriving my mother of a traditional Iranian marriage.

She also didn't like that I was marrying a foreigner, an Arab, and a Muslim. Even though her mother was a Muslim, she didn't have a high opinion of the faith. But her main objection was that I would end up living in Egypt or the U.S. instead of Iran. Nonetheless, after Pooran's prodding, she granted her permission.

A Checkerboard of Nights and Days

Mahmoud and I had become friends gradually since we met. We were never intimate during that time because of my cultural background, where sex before marriage was forbidden. Of course, he understood and respected my feelings.

We had a small engagement party in September 1959 at the International House with our friends from all corners of the world. My three Iranian friends helped with the party. Our guest of honor was the Consul General of the Egyptian embassy.

Mahmoud and I had three marriage ceremonies. The first was a civil marriage on my birthday, Dec. 21, 1959, during winter break. Next, we had a Muslim ceremony in a mosque, followed by a Baha'i ceremony at the Baha'i Center in New York City.

After we married we moved to a one-bedroom apartment on Riverside Drive with a kitchen in the closet. It was a student's life. We were studying and writing term papers and living on spaghetti dinners instead of having a honeymoon. We spent most of our time in the library. During second semester, I got a part-time job at the library, in the international section, which I loved. Later an apartment became available in student housing and in June 1960 we moved to Bancroft Hall.

Although we had hectic lives and not much money, living in New York City was a valuable and memorable experience. We continued to socialize with students from all over the world and took advantage of the city's great cultural life. We had access to half-price student tickets through Columbia University. We visited museums, saw fantastic Broadway shows, and enjoyed great performances at The Julliard School of Music, which was within walking distance from us.

At the end of March 1960, Mahmoud and I were invited to the Iranian Embassy in
Washington, D.C. to attend a Nowruz celebration. We were elated to converse with

Princess Shahnaz, the wife of the Iranian Ambassador and daughter of the Shah of Iran.

Mahmoud told her he was from Alexandria, Egypt and she replied that her mother, Queen Fawzia, had a house there. Queen Fawzia was the sister of King Farouk of Egypt and was the first wife of the Shah. Divorced and remarried, she was now living in Egypt.

Another memorable event for us was attending the United Nations General Assembly in 1960 and hearing speeches by dozens of heads of state, including Cuba's Fidel Castro and President Nasser of Egypt. Mahmoud was representing the Arab students of Columbia University. On our way in, I noticed President Castro speaking to some Columbia University students in the hall. I didn't speak to him, but remember him as tall, young, and handsome man with a commanding presence.

New York was always unpredictable, and one incident I'll never forget is when

Mahmoud's old roommate and his wife stayed with us at our apartment for one night before they left for Syria the next day. Our friends didn't realize our neighborhood wasn't very safe. Upon their departure, the husband left his one suitcase on the street and came back upstairs to get their second suitcase. When he returned to the street the first suitcase was gone. When he went looking for it, the second one disappeared as well. They lost all of their clothes and the wife's expensive jewelry. The husband had to wire his family to ask for money to get home. We felt so sorry for them.

Fourteen

The memory of becoming a mother for the first time never fades from my mind. On October 29, 1960, at eight o'clock in the morning, I was wheeled in a hospital cot from the delivery room to the recovery room, not yet completely awake from the effects of full anesthesia. Half-drowsy, I heard a whispering voice: "You had a healthy baby girl."

I felt split in two, in body and spirit. An unusual, intense feeling came over me and tears of joy welled up in my eyes. The nurse put a small bundle—a miracle—in my arms. As I cuddled her warm body and felt her heartbeat, I experienced a love I had never known before. I looked up and saw Mahmoud standing next to my bed with sleepy eyes. He had stayed up all night in the waiting room to hear the news. He took the baby in his arms, as joyful as I was to be a parent for the first time.

My life had been transformed overnight. The day before I was a wife, a friend, and a full-time student. Mahmoud and I focused on our studies and spent most of our time in the library. Now I had a new identity—I was a mother, responsible for a new human being. She was my flesh and blood, an extension of my heritage.

A Checkerboard of Nights and Days

The night before our daughter's birth, our best friends Salah and Nana El-Arabi visited us in our small apartment in New York with their little baby girl Dana. We were planning the upcoming International House Halloween Party at Columbia University.

Salah was originally from Egypt, a chunky young man in his thirties with a full head of dark, curly hair and a dark complexion. His black and penetrating eyes belied a gentle and kind disposition. His wife Nana was German—tall with light skin, blue eyes, and beautiful blonde hair, an intense, disciplined, no-nonsense individual. Their little girl Dana was the most beautiful child I had ever seen—she had a moon-shaped face, light brown skin, wavy blonde hair, and large hazel eyes, a mix of her Aryan, Arab and Semitic heritage. Salah and Nana were planning to return to Egypt, Salah to teach at the American University of Cairo and Nana was going to be a stay-home mother. Nana had converted to Islam and was applying for Egyptian citizenship; she loved Egypt. She was like a sister to me, and before they left the country they both helped me enormously with my new baby daughter.

After three days in the hospital, we brought home our precious daughter Roya (meaning "one who has a great vision for the world"). In Persian culture names have great significance and I hoped my little girl would be a visionary and a dreamer.

As new parents, we now forgot ourselves and put our daughter's needs first. We became fatigued, as Roya was a poor sleeper. Mahmoud would rock her for hours on his lap until she nodded off, only to have her awake again as soon as he put her in the crib. Then I had to walk her around the room until she finally fell asleep again. Our sleep deprivation was compounded by our efforts to keep up with our demanding student schedule.

Motherhood was a confusing and difficult for me because of the legacy of my childhood in Iran. I felt guilty because I didn't want to leave Roya with a babysitter as my parents had left me and my siblings with nannies, but I didn't have a choice. As graduate students, Mahmoud and I had heavy course loads, little money, and we didn't have any relatives nearby who could give my child the love and attention she deserved. I had to figure out how to be a mother without much guidance. One of my friends who had children gave me a book to read. The author, Dr. Benjamin Spock, was considered the foremost expert in child rearing. I read it cover to cover, desperately trying to implement some of his suggestions.

Most parents bring up their children the way they were brought up, but I didn't want to raise Roya the way I had been raised. We hadn't had the kind of parenting that I saw in America among the families I visited. My friends gave their babies and children so much love and affection. Maybe it was our circumstances or the kind of parents we had, but they did not readily express their emotions or affection openly. I vowed to give Roya the affection and attention I hadn't received.

But it wasn't easy for us. Although we were overjoyed with having a child, it was a very tough time. I had my hands full taking 12 credits of graduate courses. Roya often needed more care and attention than we could give because she was such a poor sleeper. We were up most nights rocking her. It was difficult for new parents like us to find the right balance.

Luckily, Mahmoud and I weren't completely on our own. We had a support system from other new mothers in our student housing complex, who helped with babysitting. Salah and Nana were always ready to help, psychologically and physically. With their help, Mahmoud and I managed to survive being parents and full-time graduate students at the same time, as our lives, while still hectic, became less overwhelming.

In May 1961 Mahmoud and I received overwhelming news from the Iranian consulate in New York. The Iranian government would not be renewing my scholarship because I had married someone from a different country. The news was maddening. I already had completed all course requirements for the Doctor of Education program (ED.D.), and obtained certification as a college teacher of education and psychology, but I needed at least six more months to research, write, and complete my dissertation. But how would I do that without financial support? Mahmoud and I needed the money more than ever, now that we were parents.

My husband was in the process of applying for graduate assistantships and was fortunate to receive an offer from Syracuse University, where he could work with Dr. Donald Adams, Professor of International and Cultural Education. We decided to take advantage of the opportunity and moved to Syracuse, New York.

We arrived in Syracuse and rented a small two-bedroom, second-floor apartment, within walking distance from the Syracuse University campus. Roya was just five months old.

I felt like I was starting all over again with an infant child in a new and unfamiliar city. I didn't know my way around and it was somewhat disorienting. Winter was coming and Syracuse was extremely cold. As always, Mahmoud tried to manage our lives with very limited finances. His graduate assistantship was paying him only $200 a month, and that wasn't enough to support us. I couldn't work because I had to care for Roya. It is a common predicament that many families find themselves in, even today.

It was one of the most difficult and stressful periods of my life. I had left behind my friends and support network in New York City, and the loneliness and isolation in Syracuse were unbearable. Much of the time, I was depressed and lost in my own thoughts. Tears often poured from my eyes. In Iranian culture, all female relatives come to help you after the birth of a child. In Syracuse I didn't have a single close friend, let alone family. For the first time in America I felt completely helpless.

At one point, I thought I would appeal to the Iranian government about the scholarship because I wanted to finish my dissertation. But I realized I couldn't make the bureaucratic Iranian government change its policy. I had never liked the way the Royal Scholarships had been handled. We hadn't signed a contract and it wasn't clear whether we were legally required to return to Iran after we completed our studies; nevertheless, I thought they were expecting us to go back. If I hadn't gotten married, my plan was to return to Iran, not to live there permanently, but to teach for a year or two to fulfill my obligation.

Thus, I knew the time had come to make a difficult decision. I told Mahmoud that it might be better for me to return to Iran for a year. I could get a college teaching position and my family could help with Roya. Mahmoud was reluctant, but I convinced him it would be better for him not to worry about us for a while and concentrate on his studies. As an immigrant, he had to work twice as hard to prove himself. Being a naturally optimistic person, he told me, "Don't worry Iran, life will be better for us eventually. We will make it together as a family in America!"

Finally, we agreed that I would go back to Iran to teach and give Mahmoud some space to settle down. The plan was after one year, Roya and I would return to the U.S., hopefully to an improved financial situation. The government paid for my return flight home and informed me that they had a college teaching position waiting for me.

Fifteen

In July 1961, I flew from New York to Tehran, a 12-hour flight with ten-month-old Roya. My family welcomed us at the airport, exhilarated to see us. My mother and Manoochehr were now living in a big three-story house in the northern part of the city, not far from the University of Tehran. We entered a gated courtyard surrounded by four-foot walls lined with red-flowered fire trees. The courtyard had the traditional pool in its center with flower and vegetable gardens surrounding it. My sister Pooran was working as a principal in an all-girls high school. She lived on the first floor with her husband Vali, her four-year-old son Vafa, and their young maid Fatima. Manoochehr and my mother lived on the second floor, but he was away most of the time overseeing the construction of water dams in the city of Hamadan. The project was part of the Point Four Program, a major foreign policy priority of President Truman, which assisted developing countries with their economic and technical needs. Mother rented the third floor to a young American man who spoke Farsi fluently and worked as a translator. This delightful young man used to recite Persian jokes to us and had us all laughing all the time.

After a week, I met with an administrator from the Iranian Ministry of Higher Education and applied for my teaching job. I was told I had to wait until a teaching position opened at one of the universities. I had the sense that the wait would be indefinite.

My mother and Pooran were a big help with Roya and gave me some much needed relief. They taught her some Farsi words, and my daughter enjoyed the warm and nurturing environment. She especially loved fresh Persian thin bread, just as I had so many years before when I had watched Zohreh and Sakinea bake it in my grandmother's courtyard. Roya would sit in her high chair and ask for "naan, naan!" as soon as she smelled it. She also loved Fatima, the young maid, who would play with her, tell her stories, sing to her in Persian, and put her down for naps.

Years later, Fatima told me the story of how she ended up in Tehran with my sister's family. She was a young village girl who had previously worked for my sister in Tabriz. "Pooran, my khanum (boss), didn't take me with her to Tehran," she said. "She didn't want to uproot me and left me with another family when she moved. In the meantime I ended up working for a third family that brought me to Tehran. I planned to leave this family all along. I knew Pooran was in the city but I didn't know her address; all I knew was that her husband worked for the National Bank of Iran. One day I asked my employer if he would take me to visit Mr. Vali Mogharabi at the bank."

Then Pooran told me her version: "One day my old maid Fatima appeared on my doorstep with my husband Vali. She said, 'I want to stay with you. I don't want to go back to that other family anymore.' I was so surprised. How was an illiterate 15-year-old village girl who couldn't read or write able to find us in a big city like Tehran? As it turned out, my previous household helper had left the week before and I needed help. Fatima's return was a godsend to me."

Irandukht Vahidi Fahmy

Although I cherished being reunited with my family, I became extremely discouraged by my career situation in Iran. Not only was I unemployed, but I felt even more a stranger in my native land than I had when I departed four years before. More than ever I didn't belong to that culture and environment.

The country had advanced economically since I left but remained very backward politically. Inefficiency and corruption were as rampant as ever. Everyone seemed obsessed with making money; maybe that had always been the case, but I hadn't been aware of it. And the religious hypocrisy hadn't disappeared. Some leaders in the Muslim community acted pious in public and then frequented nightclubs with alcohol and nude dancers—in Iran, in 1961, of all places! The society's values were completely imbalanced. They wanted to become Westernized, but had an incomplete picture of Western culture, sometimes mirroring the wrong values.

I had found the Iranian culture difficult long before I left the country, but now my attitude was compounded by my taste of freedom, personal responsibility and women's rights in the U.S. The so-called freedom I found on my return to Iran was not true freedom. The liberation they assumed they had wasn't authentic. I found it impossible to readjust.

I didn't enjoy the social life in Iran, where it was hard to figure out what people really meant. They said one thing but really meant something else. In Iran, and most Middle Eastern countries, the unwritten custom of "Taarof" prevailed, where people initially refused a courtesy being offered, but actually really desired it. Merchants would offer you a cup of tea when you entered their shops, but out of politeness you had to refuse the offer, accepting it only after the shopkeeper insisted several times. Refusal was a fundamental part of Iranian etiquette and a difficult concept for Westerners to understand. After becoming accustomed to the direct and plainspoken way of communicating in the U.S., I found this custom even more irritating than I had in the past.

When my mother eventually came to Syracuse to visit us a few years later, my friends had us over for lunch. They asked my mother if she would like something to drink and she refused. After she waited for a while she asked me, "What happened to the tea?"

I said, "Mother, you told them no and there's no Taarof this country. If you say no when they offer you food or drink in America, you won't get it." After several such episodes my mother learned to say "Yes, thank you" when someone offered her food or drink.

While I was in Tehran we went to visit one of the museums and a male friend drove us. We were going to have breakfast beforehand, so I asked him to join us.

"No thank you," he replied. "I don't want to trouble you."

By that time I had already become acculturated to American ways and told him:

"No. Nonsense. Please sit down and have breakfast with us."

While in Iran I returned to Rezaiyeh to visit my childhood home. I was stunned to see that it had been converted into a bank. The exterior was nothing like I remembered it; if I hadn't known I once lived there I never would have recognized it. The entire street had changed as well; the neighbors we once knew were gone. Only the little café next door was familiar. I asked my uncle, "What happened to the gardens?"

"In the beginning, after you sold the house," he said, "they still had all those fruit trees. My son and I used to go and pick the fruits all the time. But, unfortunately, they cut down the trees. You don't want to see what the courtyard looks like now."

That was devastating to hear. I thought of the endless days we spent there, of the times my siblings and I climbed the cherry trees, which seemed so impossibly tall and provided us with so much joy.

Sixteen

The college teaching job in Iran never materialized, and Mahmoud missed us tremendously and wanted us back in Syracuse. So, after three months, Roya and I returned to the U.S. on my student visa, where hopefully I would be able to finish my degree.

My husband was thrilled to see us. When he met us at the airport he opened his arms to take Roya from me but she refused to go to him and started crying. Apparently, she was very angry at having been separated from her loving and caring father. Roya's reaction tore my heart apart, and I realized that it had not been a good decision to separate my daughter from her father.

While spending those three months in Tehran, I found out I was expecting our second child, and upon my return to the U.S., I shared the good news with Mahmoud. He was elated as we welcomed our son Raef on May 3, 1962. His name means "the compassionate one" in Arabic. We were overjoyed to add a son to our family. He had a full head of black hair; but unfortunately, like Roya, he didn't sleep well. He was a very colicky baby who would stay up most of the night and needed a great deal of attention.

Now I had two babies, just 18 months apart. Mahmoud and I decided to move to the Married Student Housing at Syracuse University, which was remodeled army barracks. We had two bedrooms, a living room, and a small kitchen. Rent was $50 a month. The atmosphere was much friendlier; everyone living there was in the same situation as us: married students with small children trying to juggle all the demands that life presented. We managed to get by on very little money by helping each other, and babysitting one another's kids.

Our neighbors were from Eastern European and various Middle Eastern countries. Our best friends were from Iraq and had children the same age as Roya and Raef; they still live in Syracuse and we consider them life-long friends. We socialized and had picnics together. While I was much happier with our situation, I still felt unsatisfied, even useless at times. I loved my children with all my heart, yet I wanted to be more than a mother. I had so much education and I was doing nothing with it professionally. Since I was a teenager, my goal had been to teach and I still longed to complete my degree and fulfill my career goals.

I have seen the same desire for educational achievement in my children and grandchildren. It is not at all surprising to me that all three of my children have graduate degrees. They all inherited my love for education, which I inherited from my paternal grandfather. In fact, my grandfather embedded a love of education in my brain: "You have to be educated," he would tell me, "you have to go for the highest education."

That's why I was so disappointed when I couldn't finish my dissertation. It brought back memories of my grandfather and all he had meant to me. I felt I had failed him, that I had failed myself. Getting that degree had been so important to me that giving up my dream of becoming a professional woman bothered me for a long time afterwards.

One day when I was alone at home with the two babies, Roya touched the heater, burned her fingers and burst into tears. Raef heard Roya's cries and began to cry himself. Nobody was around to help and I had two crying babies on my hands for hours. I didn't know what to do. Finally, one of the neighbors came by to ask what was going on. He took Roya and calmed her down while I gave my attention to Raef.

After this incident, I wrote to my mother, asking if she could come to Syracuse to help me with the children. She agreed, and came to live with us for a few months. She was able to babysit the children while I worked three mornings a week at Syracuse University's library. It helped us tremendously by easing our financial burden and giving me a sense of purpose. Gradually, I made more friends in Syracuse, and was able to socialize more which in turn gave me a stronger support system, thus my mother returned home to Iran.

I loved working at the library, but also faced my first real encounter with prejudice since coming to the U.S. The head librarian was a very rude and inconsiderate person. She often insulted my intelligence and treated me like her servant, ordering me to dust the books, even though I had more education that she did and had worked in libraries before. I was so upset by the treatment she subjected me to that I came home crying. No one had ever insulted me like that before! One day, when I went to the restroom during work hours, she became enraged at me and screamed: "Where have you been? I've been calling for you and you disappeared!" I was so miserable that I quit right then and there. I could not help but feel she treated me terribly because I was an immigrant from another country who had more education that she and was striving for a better life in America.

Our third child and second daughter, Randa, was born February 4, 1964, exactly six years to the day when Mahmoud arrived in America. When I knew it was time for me to deliver the baby, we called our Egyptian friend and his wife to babysit Roya and Raef while we left for the hospital. After I gave birth, Mahmoud and I couldn't think of a name for our new little girl. We tried to find a name that began with "R", similar to Roya and Raef. One of Mahmoud's dearest friends, Ahmed El-Dersh, came to visit the new baby in the hospital and we told him we hadn't decided yet on a name. He said he had a good friend whose daughter was named Randa, which means "flowering desert tree." We loved the name and chose it immediately.

Randa was the easiest child to take care of. She slept all night, she didn't cry much, and was very calm. She followed Roya and Raef around to learn from them and at the same time had a very independent spirit. She was always smiling, happy and optimistic, traits she inherited from her father.

Within a span of five years we now had three children. Although I was much better adjusted now than when we first arrived in Syracuse, my mother was a little worried about me juggling three children, and returned to the U.S. from Iran for another four month visit. Once again, she was a big help, and cooked a lot of delicious Persian food while babysitting the children. Mahmoud would tease me by saying that my cooking was not "real Persian cooking." My mother's cooking was the real thing and we loved having her with us.

But, being in the U.S. was hard for my mother because she didn't speak English. She complained about being lonely.

"Where are all the people?" my mother would ask. "Why don't they knock on the door and visit you?"

"Everybody is so busy in this country," I told her. "Mother, in American culture people don't come without an invitation. I will invite some friends during the weekend."

She was happy to be visiting us, but never really felt comfortable in the U.S. Partly it was her age, and partly it was the vast cultural difference between Iran and the U.S. compounded by the language barrier.

After four months of visiting us in Syracuse, my mother then went to visit Bahman, who was now working in Erie, Pennsylvania, as an engineer. At that point Roya and Raef were in nursery school, and Randa stayed with a babysitter while I worked as a tutor for undergraduate Iranian students at Syracuse University. I also directed the university's Head Start program, which provided assistance to families with small children.

During our years in Syracuse, the university's dean helped us to convert our student visas to permanent residency, which meant a great deal to us. We now had all the rights and privileges of an American citizen, except for voting rights. Then, after five years of permanent residency, we could obtain our American citizenship, which would be accepted all over the world except in the country of my birth—Iranian law would not accept my change of citizenship. It didn't matter to me because I had no intention of returning to Iran.

In January 1965, my husband was offered a position to teach at Bucknell University, so we moved to Lewisburg, Pennsylvania to accept the position. Fortunately, the university had a co-op faculty-run nursery school. Roya and Raef were there every day for the morning session, and I had some time to spend alone with Randa.

I was invited to join the very active American Association of University Women and met so many friendly and well-educated women. We also had a Faculty Wives Club on campus where I made a lot of good friends. Luckily, we had a great support system among the faculty and spouses. We immediately bonded with one faculty family, the Heiners, who had three children the same age as ours. We spent a great deal of time together, and they always included us in their family Easter and Christmas dinners. I felt more included than ever in the American culture.

At the same time, there was a lot of friction between the university faculty and students, and the townspeople. Lewisburg was very provincial and not at all diverse. The local residents thought the university population was too liberal, and they were very prejudiced against newcomers and immigrants. It was a big disappointment in comparison with Syracuse, where the faculty, students, and community were much more diverse.

A Checkerboard of Nights and Days

During our first year at Bucknell University, Mahmoud and I sublet the house of a fellow faculty member who was on sabbatical. When they returned, we had to find a new place to live, but several owners of local homes told us openly that they wouldn't rent to "foreigners" - as they called us. In the 1960s, prejudice was out in the open and in full display in the tiny town of Lewisburg, Pennsylvania.

Even in the Faculty Wives Club, I received the clear message from some women that I was different and didn't fit in. I wasn't treated badly, but differently. I distinctly remember getting the impression that some members of the club felt superior, especially from the president of the organization. She would make comments to me about how she dressed and the kind of house she lived in to show that she lived better than I did.

Although we had friends, our family was not always made to feel welcome in the broader Lewisburg community. There was a birthday party for one of the children at the pre-school my children attended, but Roya and Raef were not invited. I thought that was odd. At the time I tried to brush it off, but to be honest - it really bothered me.

I know people were surprised when they met our family for the first time because we were well-dressed, highly educated, and worldly. They had a stereotype in their minds about what people from the Middle East or Iran should be like, and we clearly did not fit that stereotype. We accepted that this was part of our acculturation process in America.

Seventeen

In 1968 my husband was offered a teaching position at Wilkes College in Wilkes-Barre, Pennsylvania. I preferred to move to a bigger city with greater culture, diversity and more opportunities for my children. But, Mahmoud was impressed with the faculty at Wilkes College and the surrounding community in the Wyoming Valley. Thus, we bought a house in Dallas, Pennsylvania, just outside Wilkes-Barre, and moved there in August 1968.

However, the month before we moved there, the three children and I took a five-week trip to Egypt and Iran. Mahmoud stayed behind because he had committed to teaching summer session at Bucknell University. We flew from New York to Beirut, Lebanon direct on TWA. One of Mahmoud's brothers, Nabil, and his nephew, Mustafa, greeted us with glowing smiles at the Beirut airport. We stayed one night in Beirut at the beautiful, upscale St. Georges hotel overlooking the Mediterranean Sea. Beirut at that time was called "the Paris of the Middle East" and the hotel was filled with travelers, businessmen and dignitaries from all over the world.

While we were waiting in the hotel lobby to check-in, Raef was fidgety, running around in a circle, having just gotten off a long airplane ride. A nice, elegant lady who spoke English fluently told him, "You have such beautiful black eyes. Come here." But Raef ran away; he was very shy. I assumed she was an American by her perfect English language skills and accent.

After the trip, when we returned to our new home in Dallas that fall, I registered Raef for the first grade. I took him directly into his classroom to meet his teacher, who excitedly said "I remember seeing you at the St. Georges Hotel in Beirut!" It was such an unbelievable coincidence! She was the American woman in the lobby of the hotel who complimented Raef, and her name was Mrs. Ambrose. She had been visiting her daughter and son-in-law, who had a U.S Government posting in Lebanon. From that point on, Raef loved Mrs. Ambrose and his shyness melted away. Our good luck continued two years later when Randa entered the first grade at Dallas Elementary School and also had Mrs. Ambrose as her teacher.

After resting in Beirut for one day, Nabil and Mustafa made arrangements for us to fly from Beirut to Cairo by Egypt Air. Mahmoud's brother Gamal, who was a prominent naval physician, met us at the Cairo airport and drove us directly to Mahmoud's parents' house in Alexandria. That was the first time my children and I met Mahmoud's parents, my in-laws, uncles, aunts and cousins. Of the nine children in Mahmoud's family, four brothers and one sister were living in Egypt at the time. One brother was in Lebanon, another brother was a pharmacist living in Kuwait, and the oldest sister had passed away a few years before.

Meeting everyone was so exciting. We were warmly welcomed with kisses and hugs, while I apologized to them for Mahmoud's absence. During our ten-day stay in Egypt, my in-laws were so hospitable and caring that I felt completely at home.

My father-in-law, Hussein Fahmy, had a very prominent position in the Egyptian government. He spoke perfect English with a British accent. Brothers, sisters, nieces, and nephews all spoke English with us, eager to practice their language skills. Mahmoud's mother had some knowledge of French but couldn't speak English, which was frustrating for her. However, it didn't prevent her from showing her love and affection toward us. One of the few English words she learned was "eat" and we certainly did! Egyptians are famous for their hospitality, including large amounts of wonderfully delicious dishes, which they served us at every meal.

My children were four, six, and eight at the time and they had a hard time adjusting to all the Egyptian food. Fortunately, I took a lot of cereal and peanut butter with me, and they often chose to eat that instead. Mahmoud's mother was very concerned: "How come they're not eating anything? How come they're not used to eating good food?"

We had brought up our children just like other American children because we didn't want them to be different. In wanting them to be Americans, I rarely cooked Iranian or Egyptian food. We regularly had hamburgers, hot dogs, pizza, lasagna and Spaghetti-O's. They had been exposed to some aspects of Egyptian and Iranian culture, but my culture and my husband's culture wasn't embedded in them.

I explained to my Egyptian in-laws that it was easier for me to cook American food for my children because I didn't have the time to cook Iranian or Egyptian food, which consisted of complicated recipes. My in-laws were very understanding. They loved my children dearly. Yet this was an example of how my children often straddled three cultures throughout their lives, American, Egyptian, and Iranian. Back in the United States, they weren't exactly looked upon as American to many people, and to our relatives they weren't exactly Egyptian or Iranian.

Over time, all of our children would travel frequently with us throughout the Middle East and around the world. They were exposed to a great deal of different cultures and different values. This had both a positive and negative impact on them.

The positive part, of course, was being exposed to the warmth of our extended family.

When we went to Egypt, there were often more than twenty members of the family who were with us, sharing their kindness and love. Egyptians are very open in expressing their love and affection. And on my side of the family, my children always felt comfortable with their Iranian relatives. When my brothers and sister came to U.S., my children would stay with them for an extended period of time.

But difficulties arose when my children were exposed to the restrictions of the conservative cultures of Egypt and Iran. Our relatives sometimes felt our children had to behave and dress in certain ways. My mother expected them to sit quietly and listen to the adults, when all they wanted to do was run around, make noise, and have fun as all young children do. I didn't want my children to live under those kinds of restrictions. I didn't believe in disciplining my children when they were simply being themselves.

Irandukht Vahidi Fahmy

At one point in the early 1970s, Mahmoud and I considered taking a sabbatical to live in Egypt for a year. We thought the children could learn Arabic and would get to know their grandparents, uncles, aunts, and cousins better. Our internal family discussions ensued: Egypt was a more open society than Iran because they had been under British rule and were much more westernized. Egyptian Muslims weren't as conservative as Iranian Muslims. On the other hand, we considered Iran to be a more secular country under the rule of the Shah, and not a religiously ruled country. Egypt, in contrast, was a de facto Muslim country. Mahmoud's family was religious, yet very open-minded, but the society as a whole was more conservatively religious than Iran. Finally, while Mahmoud's family was wonderful, I also saw ways in which they interfered in each other's lives. I had always been an independent person, making decisions for myself.

Ultimately, we decided against the sabbatical in Egypt, due to the children's quality education in the United States. Furthermore, my children were 100% American and couldn't live in a strict, traditional culture. We would go back to visit Egypt and Iran often, but the U.S. was our home.

One of the highlights of our trip to Egypt in 1968 was a visit to the famous Egyptian Pyramids in Cairo, one of the Seven Wonders of the World. While in Cairo, we stayed with Mahmoud's maternal uncle and I was reunited with our good friends Salah and Nana, who had moved back to Egypt a few years prior with their two daughters. One day we took a tour of the old city and visited the famous Al-Azhar mosque and university, a historic divinity school for Sunni Muslim imams. We visited a bazaar called Khan-el-Khalili, where stalls were crammed with beautiful handicrafts, antiquities and famous papyrus with ancient Egyptian writing. We loved to bargain with the merchants in the bazaar, and bought many gifts for our American friends back home.

During another memorable visit to Egypt, Mahmoud's oldest brother, Sayed, was serving as the head of the Egyptian national police force. He would often drive his three children and our three children around the city in his large car with his hand constantly on the telephone in case of an emergency. My children were amazed that he had a telephone in his large Cadillac, and wondered why their father didn't have one in our car back home. They didn't realize that senior government officials, not regular people, had phones in their cars back then. Sayed later became Egypt's Minister of the Interior during President Anwar Sadat's administration.

Over the years, we would take many additional trips to Egypt, visiting the Aswan Dam, the Valley of the Kings, the Sinai, and Sharm el-Sheikh, a beautiful resort area on the Mediterranean. The beaches there are beautiful and the water is a bright aqua shade. It left me in awe to see the morning sun on those calm and glittering waters.

After our 1968 visit to Egypt, we then flew on to Tehran by British Air. My family and friends met us at the Tehran airport and took us to my mother's house. My mother was still living with Pooran's family and Manoochehr in the same three-story house.

Their standard of living had improved even more so since my last visit seven year earlier. They had all of the Western conveniences: modern appliances and automobiles. The country itself was in the midst of development and progress. Roads were improved; shopping malls and supermarkets were being built along boulevards. Parks with beautiful flowerbeds had been added to the center city. There were more museums and libraries. Foreign investment was encouraged. My brother Manoochehr was working as an engineer for an Iranian-American construction company, working side-by-side with his American counterparts building bridges and more dams.

I was pleased to hear from my sister and brother that the number of higher educational institutions had increased. New universities and colleges had opened. The most modern was Aryamehr University of Technology, the technical university of Tehran. Most of the Ph.D. faculty had been recruited from Europe and the U.S. My youngest brother Bahman, who later accepted a teaching position at Massachusetts Institute of Technology (MIT), taught mathematics and engineering at Aryamehr. He and a friend eventually started the Open and Free University of Iran, reaching out to students in rural areas who didn't have access to higher education in the big cities.

While we were in Iran in 1968, Bahman, his wife Kathy, and his two boys, Craig and Steven, flew from the United States to Europe. They rented a big van and drove through Europe to Turkey, finally meeting us in Tehran. Now my whole family was together, and we decided to take a road trip across Iran! All the adults and children climbed into the rented van and off we went through the Iranian desert to visit Esfahan, the biggest and most famous ancient city in the country. Persians call it Nesfejhan, which means "half of the world." It had been the capital of the

Persian Empire in the 17th century. I had never visited the city and was eagerly anticipating the visit.

Because it was summer vacation, Iran's Ministry of Education allowed visitors to stay in state owned school buildings. Pooran had packed some basic supplies in the van; dishes, the samovar, and mattresses. We arrived in Esfahan at night, unrolled our mattresses on the floor of a high school classroom, and had a good night's sleep. In the morning Bahman went out and bought sangak (flatbread), fresh fruit, and dense, freshly-made cream. We ate it for breakfast, along with oranges, pomegranates, feta cheese, and tea.

Esfahan was crowded with visitors, and people were practically on top of each other. Heavy loads were being drawn by animals and camels in the streets. It was an agricultural center and very self-sufficient, with most goods and food supplies coming from the surrounding villages. Esfahan has a desert climate, hot during the day and cold at night; the winters are snowy and spring is the rainy season, but the temperature is moderate. As a result, trees bloom and the gardens are full of flowers all year long. There is an old saying: "Who comes to Esfahan cannot fall ill; who comes there ill will see his health restored." We took a walking tour to see all the marvels of the city, including the Royal Square in the ancient district. We had a delicious Persian stew for lunch in a famous restaurant run by locals, and shopped for handicrafts in the bazaar.

We left Esfahan after three days and headed south on dusty, winding, and narrow desert roads to visit the famous Persepolis Palace. Even in its ruined state, it was the most stunning and monumental architecture I had seen. Destroyed during the Arab-Islamic invasion, it was rebuilt, but then burned by Alexander the Great and his victorious armies. The palace occupies a massive area five times the size of a football field. Of the original 550 columns only about a dozen are left. However, the ruins are a testament to the might of the Persian Empire and the power of ancient Persian kings. All the kings and their entourages went to Persepolis Palace to celebrate Nowruz. Reza Shah had his famous coronation at Persepolis, before he was ousted from the throne.

From there we traveled back to Tehran and enjoyed our ongoing family reunion for a few days; then Bahman, his family, Pooran, and I left to visit Tabriz, while my children stayed with my mother in Tehran. We stayed one day and one night in Tabriz, enjoying the hospitality of my cousin's wife's family. Then we went on to Rezaiyeh, where the six of us stayed with my younger uncle and his family, savored his wife's wonderful cooking, and tasted luscious fruit from my uncle's gardens and fruit trees. After a couple of days Bahman and his family drove back through Europe and returned to the U.S.

Pooran and I visited with our old friends and their families in Rezaiyeh, and we went to see our old high school principal, Zeebandeh Khanoum, a very proper, disciplined, and highly respected woman. Meeting her again after many years was a moving experience. She had always been very kind and helpful to me. She said, "Do you remember I used to tell you that you would be very successful in the future?" It was so gratifying to hear her tell me that.

Then Pooran and I walked the length of Pahlavi Avenue and stopped in front of our family home. This visit, it was no longer a bank, but a hotel. It saddened me, but not as much as when I had seen it in 1961. We gazed at it for a few moments from the sidewalk; we had no desire to go inside. When we left, I knew I would never visit my childhood home again.

When Pooran and I returned to Tehran, Manoochehr invited us to his vacation home on the Caspian Sea in the northern part of Iran, an area renowned for its splendid beauty, pleasant climate, lofty mountains, fisheries, and agriculture. The region is also famous for its sturgeon, which produces world famous Iranian caviar. My children and I enjoyed swimming in the calm and clear waters of the Caspian Sea.

After four days we returned to Tehran through mountain roads. We stopped on the way at a small roadside café owned by a husband and wife who also sold handmade arts and crafts. We enjoyed a wonderful grilled fish lunch with greens and rice grown on local farms. It was now the middle of August, and it was time for us to leave Iran and say goodbye to my family. I did not realize then that this would be my last visit to Iran. What I also couldn't have predicted was that most of my family would one day be living in the United States with me.

Eighteen

We arrived back in New York on August 20, 1968, and my husband and his brother met us at John F. Kennedy Airport. They drove us directly to our new home in Dallas, Pennsylvania. While we were away in Egypt and Iran, Mahmoud and his brother moved all of our belongings into our new home, and it looked beautiful when we entered for the first time. The children were so excited to see their brand new beautiful house with a large front and back yard. We immediately had to get the children ready for school; Roya was going into third grade, Raef was starting first grade, and Randa was starting nursery school.

During this busy time, I received a telephone call from Dr. Milford Barnes, the Director of the Children's Service Center in Wilkes-Barre, a diagnostic and treatment center for children with mental health and developmental challenges. He had heard that Mahmoud accepted a full-time position with Wilkes College and had an equally talented wife with a graduate degree in special education. They had an immediate opening for an educator and he wanted me to apply for the position. The job description sounded perfect: I would be working on a team with a nurse, psychologist, and social worker. I applied and was immediately offered the job. Thus, I began a wonderful career at the Children's Service Center on North Franklin Street in Wilkes-Barre, Pennsylvania, conveniently located three blocks from Wilkes College, where my husband worked. I finally felt like it was all coming together, and that I would be able to both raise a family and excel in my career.

For as long as I live, I will never forget Dr. Barnes. He was a compassionate professional and a great man. When he interviewed me I told him I had three kids at home and wasn't sure I could manage the job. "Don't worry about it," he said. "You'll get all the help you need to make this work." I didn't know anything about working with emotionally challenged children, but it was the best learning experience I could possibly have had.

Nor will I ever forget the kindness of the people I worked with. The center cook who made lunch for the children would always say to me, "Mrs. Fahmy, please don't forget about your lunch. I have such a delicious meal for you."

"But I brought my lunch," I would tell her.

"No, you're eating my lunch. This is especially made for you."

And, of course, I will never forget the children I worked with.

In my second year at the Center a little boy named Eric joined our program. I had been told in advance that he was nine years old, but when he walked into the room he looked less than half that age; he had very small features. His diagnosis was dwarfism.

During our case review of Eric, the psychologist told me he was a smart child, that his problems were both developmental and psychological. When he was two years old and started running around the house, as toddlers do, his single mother had chained him to his crib. Her rationalization for this was that Eric wouldn't hurt himself, but the mother obviously had some kind of psychological problems of her own. Eric's grandmother reported the abuse to child welfare and Eric was placed in a foster home. He came to the Center for day services.

Understandably, Eric was a very difficult child to handle. He was constantly running around and screaming. He had no communication skills and we never knew what he wanted. The only way he could express himself was through temper tantrums.

The first thing we did for Eric was provide him with a lot of love. Then I had to calm him down because he was extremely high-strung. "Eric," I would tell him, "just breathe."

If he became angry, I had a selection of toys he could pick from. I would ask him, "Do you like your toy? What is it about this toy that you like?" He was soothed by toys that made a sound when he squeezed them. I used a lot of non-verbal strategies in working with Eric. If I put a puzzle in front of him, he would calm down and work on it diligently until he solved it, which indicated that he was intelligent. Therapists worked with his feelings about what happened to him, because he surely remembered how he had been abused in his home. So it was a process that involved a lot of socialization, working with him one-on-one, and slowly building his trust.

Eric blossomed during the three years he was in the foster home and came to the Center. He learned to read and write, and how to communicate verbally. He grew physically and his appearance greatly improved. Eric's foster father was a minister in a Presbyterian church, and the church elders helped to raise Eric. He received so much love from his foster family and the church community, and it showed in both his emotional and physical development.

Eric's foster parents wanted to adopt him, but were legally prevented from doing so because the biological mother wouldn't give her permission. Therapists and social workers met with the mother to try to change her mind, without success. She told them: "This is my child. You took him away once, and I'm not going to let you do it again." Unfortunately, she got custody of Eric, and the foster family was devastated. Today, the laws have been changed. If a child has been severely abused, it can be much easier for that child to be adopted by a loving foster family.

When Eric was returned to his biological mother, I never heard what happened to him after that. He lived two hours away and we lost touch. A supervisor from the Center was sent to Eric's home to help the mother with Eric and check on his well-being. I found out later that Eric's mother dismissed the supervisor and would not allow her to come into the house. To this day, I still think of him and wonder what happened to him.

Most of the young children had psychiatric diagnoses. Initially I worked with autistic children, but later on we had students who had behavior disorders, learning problems, and social challenges. The autistic children were very difficult to handle.

In my first year, we had six students and four staff, so we could work one-on-one. As time went on the number of students increased, and they had even more severe social, emotional, and behavioral problems. Eventually the day treatment program had a director, eight teachers, and ten support staff, plus a cook and housekeeper.

My primary role in working with autistic children was to teach them communication skills because they weren't verbal and couldn't communicate their simplest needs. We had to concentrate on teaching them behavior before they could learn anything more. They had to learn to sit down, follow directions, and act in a disciplined way before they could be taught to read and write.

Our team approach worked with the whole child—physically, emotionally, and educationally. You cannot teach a child any other way.

We had one autistic child, a handsome five-year-old named John. You would never suspect there was anything wrong with him, but he couldn't communicate.

One day John was face down on the floor, screaming and crying. "John," I kept saying, "what's wrong? Tell me." I called our staff physician, Dr. Harris, who was able to determine that John had a terrible stomachache. But the child didn't have the ability to communicate that to us. Later on we taught autistic children sign language so they could express their feelings. During the 1970s and 80s there was very little information about autism. therefore we had to educate ourselves about it through our own research.

I worked with another autistic child who was very bright but wouldn't say a word. Yet, if you put a large jigsaw puzzle in front of him with a hundred different pieces, he would complete it in a half hour.

Many autistic children also suffer from obsessive-compulsive disorder, which is an obsession with certain behaviors, rituals, or objects. His obsession was peanut butter. He didn't want to eat anything else. We would hide it from him to teach him to ask for it. Perhaps asking for peanut butter all the time was his way of being like other children. If all the other children were eating peanut butter, why couldn't he have it too?

I ran into him twenty five years later. He was now a young man and his parents had enrolled him in a special residential school in Philadelphia. When he saw me, he ran over and tugged on my shirt. I recognized him right away.

"Mrs. Fa-Fa-Fahmy!" he said. He still had communication challenges, but he had improved greatly, and he still remembered my name after all those years.

I learned so much during my time at the Children's Service Center—about how therapists and psychologists work together to help these challenged children, and, most of all, about working with other professionals as a team. For the first time, I finally had a profession in which I was able to use all my skills, experience, and education. Throughout my life, learning had been my salvation, and never did I learn more or face greater challenges than working there. I had taken special education courses, but my real education was in doing the actual work, day by day, with children who had a wide range of challenges.

Irandukht Vahidi Fahmy

There was no specific moment when I said to myself, "I'm really good at this job and I really fit in and belong." It happened gradually, over time, starting with my first year.

When the Center opened a pre-school for younger children, a new teacher named Debbie Mermelstein joined us, and we became extremely close friends. She belonged to the Jewish faith, and one holiday season she and I were invited to the Center's party to decorate their Christmas tree. Neither of us had decorated a Christmas tree before.

"You want us—a Jew and a Baha'i—to decorate the tree?" Debbie asked, laughing.

"Yes," one of the social workers said, "don't worry, we trust you. Here are the decorations."

Debbie and I were inseparable, sharing each other's family joys, sorrows and challenges. Our children and husbands became close friends as well. My children always remember her famous chocolate cake recipe, which included chocolate pudding and chocolate chips. They had a special name for it: "My Best Friend's Chocolate Cake." She eventually retired in Florida, and we keep in touch several times a year.

My husband, children, and I were invited to every social event at the Center, whether it was Christmas, birthday parties, or weddings. I was so happy to work there, not only to contribute financially to the family, but also to use my education to its fullest. Eventually, my responsibilities at the Center greatly increased, and it became extremely challenging to balance my professional life with three school-age children. My husband was teaching night classes and lecturing, trying to help out around the house as much as he could. As always, Mahmoud had the right attitude: "Look at us now Iran! I told you things would get better for us in America – and they have."

My career at the Children's Service Center also helped with my acculturation to the United States, more than any other experience I had. I worked with parents who were very well to do, and with parents who were desperately struggling financially. I worked with highly educated parents; I worked with parents who hadn't graduated from high school. I worked with psychologists and psychiatrists, and with the cooks and janitors on our staff. For the first time I worked as a professional team member with other professionals. In Iran, I never worked with people as a team; people there worked individually in their jobs and teamwork didn't exist. And, of course, I worked with children who suffered from every conceivable type of social and emotional challenge.

It led me to the conclusion that you don't become acculturated to American life by spending time with people who are exactly like you. Mahmoud had a wonderful professional career working with outstanding colleagues. He moved in intellectual circles, among college professors and faculty. But he was also involved in many community activities that allowed him to meet people of various backgrounds. I worked closely with people from all walks of life, from every race, ethnicity, social class, and economic group. It was the best education I ever had. Not only did I have the opportunity to use my skills to the fullest and master new ones, but also had to learn to work collaboratively with people who were far different from me. There is nothing more American than that kind of diverse learning experience.

Irandukht Vahidi Fahmy

And there is nothing more American than the kindness, patience and hospitality of the American people. I truly experienced that throughout my life in the United States, but in particular from my colleagues, staff, parents, and children at the Children's Service Center, who truly taught me the lessons of tolerance, inclusion, kindness, patience and persistence.

.

Nineteen

My husband and I had always intended to raise our children as true Americans who would be assimilated 100% into the U.S. We intentionally gave them somewhat easier names to pronounce, unlike mine and my husband's. We didn't teach our children other languages; they had to learn English first. In wanting them to be Americans, we regularly ate hamburgers, hot dogs, and Spaghetti-O's more often than Iranian or Egyptian food. We even had a pet dog named Snowball. She was a black and white English-Springer Spaniel mix and was a birthday present for Raef. We all pitched in to take care of her and she quickly became part of our family.

Roya and Randa were involved in Girl Scouts, chorus, cheerleading, and various community activities. Raef was active in the Boy Scouts, and played football, baseball, and basketball. Raising first generation American children with strict Middle Eastern values and traditions would have been a big mistake. Yet as much as I wanted to raise our children differently from how I had been raised, and as much as I wanted their experiences to be different from my own, we couldn't avoid family conflicts that stemmed from our ingrained cultural biases.

Irandukht Vahidi Fahmy

The first time I experienced real difficulties with Roya was when she became a pre-teen and began menstruating. She came to me confused, but it was so hard for me to discuss how her body was changing because my mother had never discussed it with me. In Iran, any discussion related to sexuality was taboo. Luckily, I had an aunt who was as young as I was and could explain it to me.

Instead of talking to Roya, I gave her a book to read. I wasn't avoiding the issue; I simply didn't feel comfortable talking about my own experience. Part of the reason I gave her a book was that Roya loved to read. Once she got in trouble with one of her teachers for reading novels in the back of the classroom. Clearly, my response was somewhat unsympathetic. Looking back, I would have handled it differently. I would hug her and say, "Oh my, you're growing into a young woman," instead of saying, "You'll be okay, here's a book."

Due to our Middle Eastern values, I think Mahmoud and I were probably harder on Roya as our first-born and first teenager than we were with the other children. I had differences of opinion with Roya about how she should behave, dress, and speak. I was dressing her up in beautiful outfits while she wanted to wear bellbottoms and t-shirts like everybody else. Once again, I was trying to raise her as I had been raised. As a child I was always dressed up.

This was not a new struggle with Roya. When we were living in Syracuse, I dressed Roya in a beautiful woolen skirt and a pretty blouse, an outfit that was a gift from my mother. Like most three-year-olds would do, she went out and jumped in the sandbox with her beautiful outfit. When she came home she had sand all over her and I was extremely upset. I said, "Oh My God, you ruined your beautiful clothes!"

She just looked at me and kept apologizing: "I'm sorry, mom. I'm sorry." Now, I feel terrible about that, but I was raising her the way I had been raised.

After Roya was born I had two more children in the following three and a half years, so Roya didn't have much time to be a child. With three children in the family, she didn't get as much attention as she needed.

We loved her as much as our other children, but perhaps we didn't tell her that enough or praise her enough. I was unable to praise my children because I had never been praised by my parents. If one of our children brought home a C, Mahmoud and I would demand, "Why didn't you do better?" instead of saying, "That's okay, you did the best you could. Maybe next time you'll do better."

When Raef was in the ninth grade he got a C in mechanical drawing. He covered it with ink on his report card and I noticed it right way. He told me he was afraid that his father would be upset with him. And he was.

We didn't directly tell our children that they had to get good grades; they simply got the feeling from us that educational achievement was expected. It wasn't easy for Raef because he was the only son and Mahmoud expected a lot from him, which is customary in Middle Eastern culture.

We also had conflicts with our children over their social lives. Roya saw her friends dating and she knew that was out of the question for her. We made it very clear to our children that they could bring friends over to the house, but dating was out of the question until college.

When she was in the eighth grade, Roya asked if she could visit a friend's house in the evening. They were neighbors who lived two doors down and I gave her permission. "You can stay for a while," I told her. "Just call me before you walk home."

When she got back, I asked her, "How was it?"

"Oh, my friend's mother went out with her boyfriend and left us alone," Roya said. She was bewildered and frightened.

I was so upset that I didn't let her visit friends' houses anymore. To me, the mother was immoral and irresponsible to leave two young children alone like that.

During her high school years, I thought Roya was very successful and popular. She was in the honors society, was respected by her teachers, and was a cheerleader. Unbeknownst to me, she thought she wasn't attractive because she didn't have blonde hair and blue eyes. I continued to praise her academics, not realizing she only wanted to be called beautiful.

When she got older, Roya referred to herself as a "third culture kid." Because I was Iranian and her father was Egyptian, she considered those to be the cultures she was born into. Her third and adopted culture is as an American. She never felt she was as American as other first generation children. She related better to people from other cultures. Growing up, she felt misunderstood by her peers, and always somewhat out of place in the U.S. She simply didn't feel as much at home here in America as she would have liked.

I think this issue affected Raef and Randa much less, and one reason for that was that Mahmoud and I were much more acculturated to American life when they were born. They were less influenced by our Middle Eastern backgrounds than Roya was.

Raef tells me he doesn't recall feeling different or excluded as a young boy. He spent hours on end playing outside with the neighborhood boys and exploring the woods that were near our home. He enjoyed our multiple trips to Iran and Egypt, and would chuckle whenever his Egyptian cousins would tell him, "You look Egyptian but you're 'Amrikin.'"

As Raef grew into adolescence, his trips to the Middle East and Europe transformed his views of the U.S. He gained a greater appreciation for the abundance of wealth and convenience concentrated in this country compared to the third world. As he matured, he became less tolerant of the complaints that most Americans have about life's trivial inconveniences. He had seen the struggles and sacrifices by third world populations, and they accepted these struggles, sometimes with great dignity. This caused a major transformation in his perspective during his teenage and young adult years.

The vast majority Raef's friends in high school had never travelled out of the U.S. or even Pennsylvania. He realized as a very young man that there was so much more to experience and learn about beyond his small town in Pennsylvania. Raef craved deeper conversations and connections with people, revolving around world events, music, art, and politics.

Irandukht Vahidi Fahmy

It was difficult for him to understand the importance his peers attached to relationship breakups, what car you owned, sporting rivalries, football, NASCAR, hunting season, the kind of rifle you owned, and how much beer you could drink at night in the woods. His father and I didn't drink or smoke, practiced separate religions, never owned a firearm, and enjoyed quiet weekends at home.

But, like most adolescents, Raef wanted to fit in and be a "normal high school teen," so he took the best from both worlds. He learned to love football and basketball and lettered in three varsity sports. While he never learned how to hunt, or owned a firearm, he taught himself how to fish. He drove a red 1973 Camaro, dated girls, and socialized with a solid group of male and female friends. He "got hammered" for the first time on his high school graduation night, laughed when his friends mimicked his parents' accents and phrases, and quietly smiled when his coaches called him "the crazy Arab." He read *The New York Times* on Sunday, then watched the NFL.

He embraced respect and manners, learned to accept all cultures and religions, and struggled with the observance and true meaning of Christmas in our home and with religion in general. Most of all, he learned from how Mahmoud and I gradually accepted American culture and in turn were accepted by it.

Randa says she remembers, with pride, how grateful Mahmoud and I were to be in the U.S., and that this had a huge impact on her. She always felt fully American, maybe even more so that most children her age, but at the same time had an appreciation for her parents' two homelands. As a child, she was so grateful that Mahmoud and I celebrated all the "American" holidays: Christmas, Valentine's Day, Easter, Fourth of July, Halloween, and Thanksgiving.

One of her earliest memories was of Mahmoud and I being sworn in as U.S. citizens. She was right by our side as we raised our hands to take the oath. Another was of our Fourth of July celebrations in our small town of Dallas, Pennsylvania where she would ride her red, white, and blue Sears bicycle through the streets of our neighborhood yelling "Happy Birthday America!" She would often remove the battery powered radio from the handlebars of that Sears bike, and sneak it into her bedroom at night, where under her covers she would listen to incoming election results from local, state and federal political races until well past midnight. She loved when we would travel around the U.S., especially to Washington, D.C., where she was mesmerized by the White House and Mount Vernon, President George Washington's home. When she was in college, she secured a summer internship in Washington, D.C. with Pennsylvania's United States Senator John Heinz, who told her "One day you will be sitting in my seat." She eventually moved to the nation's capital to attend law school, practice law, and work in the U.S. Senate and the White House.

Like Roya and Raef, she always felt a special gratitude for America because of what she had seen during her travels with us throughout the world. Knowing what other countries were like, she could fully appreciate their cultures, language, food, and customs, yet always knew that America was the best country in the world.

One of Randa's favorite sayings is, "There but for the grace of God go I." She knows she would have never been able to pursue her career in law and politics in Washington, D.C. if she had been raised in Iran or Egypt. Now, as a lawyer, she often implements U.S. law and policy at home and abroad. She has the utmost respect for those laws and policies because of her exposure to other cultures and societies.

Perhaps, in a way, my children are more American than the average citizen because they know first-hand what other countries are like. Because they have something to compare their country with, they love America even more as a result.

Yet as much as my children love this country, and as much as Mahmoud and I love it, I always knew that the United States, with all its strengths, also had some weaknesses. One day Roya came home from the playground in tears and asked me, "Mom, what's a nigger? Am I one?" How could I explain this to my five-year-old daughter, who had brown skin?

I told her that some children were ignorant, misguided and uninformed. I did the best I could to explain what the word meant and what prejudice and racism were. I explained the historical nature of slavery in America: how people from Africa were brutally forced to come to America as slaves and faced so many barriers and discrimination as they fought for their freedom in America. I told her that unfortunately, discrimination still remains, but that America was a place where people did not judge you by the color of your skin. But even as I consoled her, I knew my words weren't enough. It was very hard for the both of us to understand why she had been treated that way by the other children.

A Checkerboard of Nights and Days

When I first came to America in the 1950s the Civil Rights struggle was ongoing. There were very few people of color on TV, in the newspapers or magazines, or in the American political system. They were excluded from most professions and constantly felt the effects of discrimination. There was very little understanding of or respect for diversity. Since then, American has made some progress, but much more still needs to be done.

As an immigrant to this country with a heavy accent, I had long accepted the fact that I would often be discriminated against, misunderstood, stared at, or looked down upon. For me, it was more difficult. My heavy accent always caused problems. Every time I said my name, people would ask, "What did you say?" I had to repeat my name over and over.

In certain situations, people would talk to me slowly, spell words, and ask if I understood what they meant. I realized that when you have an accent, people think you are unintelligent. At times they didn't know how to act around me. I learned coping mechanisms to ignore them. I learned to be friendlier with people who were unfriendly toward me. If somebody reacted to me in an odd or uncomfortable way, I knew the reason for it. When people said things that weren't kind, I saw it as part of the price of living in this country.

Oddly enough, my husband Mahmoud rarely experienced these problems. Perhaps his positive attitude, outgoing personality, mastery of the English language, and confidence helped inoculate him from those negative reactions. He was accepted by the community, loved by his students, and respected for his values and opinions. His favorite saying is "I am an American by choice – you are an American by accident."

I had long accepted that I would have to work twice as hard as any American to fit in and to achieve success, but my children should not have to. They always considered themselves American. Thus, it was hard for my children when people reacted in odd ways or treated them differently. Roya looks very Middle Eastern and people would always ask where she was from. Many people assumed Randa was Hispanic, Italian or Greek. But they were fully American and therefore shocked when someone would ask "Where are you from?" or "What nationality are you?" When they asked Raef that question, he would always say, "I can be anything you want me to be."

We tried very hard to bring them up as American as we could. So much so that my mother would complain that she couldn't talk to her grandchildren in the Persian language, Farsi, but our goal was to Americanize them. I thought learning other languages would confuse them and slow down their language development.

As someone who had studied psychology, I knew and still believe that prejudice and intolerance are unfortunately part of the human psyche. I also knew that in other parts of the world, prejudice and ignorance were even worse. I grew up experiencing intolerance toward women and people of different religions that made me uncomfortable just to walk on certain streets. I had never forgotten how my friend's conservative Muslim parents smashed the glass my Baha'i friend had drank from. This was a division of both religion and class. I saw how the average Iranian treated their household help. Economically disadvantaged people in Iran would be drafted into the army; when there was no war to fight, they served as servants to the officers, cleaning bathrooms and changing their children's diapers.

Even in Europe, which is supposed to be more progressive than America, immigrants are not as accepted as they are in the United States. I have family in Europe, in Germany, England, and Italy, who tell me they have never been fully accepted as citizens. I asked my aunt, who has lived in Italy for many years and who speaks Italian fluently, "Do you have any Italian friends?" The answer was no. She said that some Italians were hesitant to even associate with her, let alone befriend her. Immigrants are simply not accepted.

In the early 1980's, Mahmoud was recruited by the local community to run for the Dallas School District's Board of Education. One night we received an anonymous telephone call: "You can't be running for the school board! You don't know anything about the school system and you're a foreigner!" This incident backfired, and strongly motivated my husband and daughter Randa, who was in high school at that time. Randa served as Mahmoud's campaign manager knocking on doors and passing out campaign literature which highlighted his PhD in Education. He not only won the seat on the school board, but also was elected President of the Board of Directors.

In the mid 1980s, when Mahmoud and I were planning to take a year-long sabbatical to Qatar, a tiny country in the Persian Gulf, we received another disturbing telephone call: "We're so happy to hear that you're leaving America and going back to your country." Who outside the family had found out about our career plans?

Had they been monitoring us, watching our every move? We knew that extremist groups were active in Pennsylvania and one had headquarters within eight miles of where we lived. Furthermore, Qatar was not "our country." America is! We dismissed the caller, but it was a continuous reminder that our struggle to become fully American was ongoing.

Over time, Mahmoud and I changed our approaches to parenting. We became less rigid and more open-minded. We let our children have some more freedom and a few more choices.

I had minored in psychology, which helped me understand how my childhood had affected my way of thinking. I began to realize that I couldn't raise my children the way I had been raised and that I had to change. Roya grew up to believe that I expected perfection from her. She felt she could never live up to my expectations. We've both come to understand that I did expect too much of her. Over many years we've slowly learned that there is no such thing as perfection and that children should be allowed to develop their own personalities. I did not have that freedom as a child, but as a mother I had to learn to grant it to my children. As my husband and I became more assimilated in American culture, our outlook toward life changed. We tried very hard to erase the divide that separates foreign born parents from their American children, but the reality is that it can never be erased.

It wasn't just that Mahmoud and I were changing. The entire country was changing, and we were changing along with it.

Mahmoud and I are proud that Roya, Raef, and Randa have grown up to be valuable and devoted members of their respective communities. We're so pleased to see how our three children treat their own children with respect and love. They indeed learned the most important values that we tried so hard to teach them.

My advice to my children has always been to live your life day by day. The past is gone and the future has not arrived, so we should live as best we can in the present moment, as Omar Khayyám reminds us:

> *Ah, fill the Cup —what boots it to repeat*
> *How Time is slipping underneath our Feet:*
> *Unborn to-morrow and dead yesterday,*
> *Why fret about them if to-day be sweet!*

Twenty

In 1979 the Iranian Islamic Revolution swept the country. Mahmoud and I were shocked as we watched a secular nation transform into a fundamentalist Muslim country. We assumed if there was going to be a revolution against the Shah of Iran, it would be a nationalist revolution, not a religious one. To see the country taken over by the Ayatollah Khomeini and his religious zealots who established Sharia law, and the taking of 52 American hostages for 444 days, was disheartening and demoralizing for our country and our family.

During that time, very few Americans understood the complicated political history of U.S.-Iranian bilateral relations dating back to the 1950s, which eventually led to the Islamic Revolution. In its anti-communist zeal, the U.S. CIA covertly supported the 1953 coup in Iran, which deposed the democratically elected socialist prime minister Mohammad Mosaddegh, and allowed the Shah of Iran to regain the throne. The Shah's government was very loyal to America, but was internally corrupt. His secret police detained and tortured opposition figures and religious dissidents over the many years. As a result, many Iranian harbored resentment since 1953, and that resentment grew through the years until it exploded into a full blown revolution in 1979.

A Checkerboard of Nights and Days

At first, we held out hope that the Islamic Revolution might be good for Iran. Perhaps it would lead to the establishment of a democratic government. But as the weeks and months went by, we watched the situation gravely deteriorate.

Before I came to America, Iranians were solidly pro-American. America represented freedom, opportunity, and the most advanced culture in the world. During the revolutionary period, I would speak with some Iranians who continued to express their admiration for the American people and its culture. Unfortunately, the Islamic Republic's religious zealots spread their negative propaganda, and became very intolerant of the U.S., forcing crowds to chant "Death to America."

It was very upsetting for me personally, because my mother, Manoochehr, Pooran, and their families were still in in Iran. Although Bahman lived in the U.S., he happened to be visiting Iran at that time, but decided to leave the country on the very day the Ayatollah Khomeini arrived in Tehran. It was a very unsettling and worrisome time for all of us. We despised the Islamic revolutionary government for what they did to the country. The very people who I had disliked as a child were now in power.

Mahmoud and I decided we needed to get all of my family out of Iran. We knew they were in danger due to their political beliefs and religious minority status as Baha'is. So we proceeded to sponsor all of them through the U.S. Immigration and Naturalization Service. Fortunately, my sister Pooran and her family were the first to arrive in 1980. Next, we succeeded in getting Manoochehr's son Virasb out of Iran and into the U.S. He came to live with us in Dallas, Pennsylvania and attended Wilkes College with my daughter Randa. A year later, we were able to get his sister Mahsa out. However, my brother Manoochehr stayed behind in Tehran to be with my mother, who always held out hope that the situation would improve.

Fortunately, we never received any negative comments, reactions or telephone calls during the Iranian hostage situation. By then we were well established in the community and everyone knew us. Mahmoud had an administrative position at Wilkes College and was active in a half-dozen community organizations. I was working as a special education teacher supervisor with twelve school districts in Luzerne County. If we weren't American by now, we would never be.

During the 1970s and again in the early 80s my mother traveled back and forth between Iran and the U.S., staying with us in Pennsylvania and with my siblings, who eventually moved to Southern California. When she was staying in California with Pooran and Bahman, my mother complained of loneliness. She couldn't speak the language and she was very unhappy. She was always a woman who was very hard to please. She had experienced very hard times, and I wonder if the depression and grief of losing her eldest son and young husband ever left her.

We tried to convince her to stay in America, but she felt strongly connected to her country, Iran, despite the political turmoil. Sadly, in 1985 she returned to Iran and passed away shortly thereafter. She had been sick, but Manoochehr thought that if she had stayed in the U.S. she might have gotten better medical care and wouldn't have died. Doctors were overwhelmed in Iran and she didn't receive the best treatment; she had a little arthritis and a heart problem, but nothing major. We wanted her to stay in the U.S. but she decided to go back.

Although she wasn't in the best of health, her death wasn't expected. I was in my office when my colleague came in to say, "Your husband just called and wants you to meet him in his office at Wilkes."

"What is it?"

I was frightened and shaken because my first thought was that something awful had happened to one of our children. When I got to his office, Mahmoud told me that Manoochehr called him to deliver the bad news: "God bless her, your mother passed away."

Her death deeply affected me, and I began to have dreams about her. She would appear in front of me saying, "Where have you gone? You have left me behind." The dreams were stirred by my guilt that when she died in Iran, I hadn't been there to comfort her. The Islamic Revolution had made it impossible for me to go back. But Manoochehr was eventually able to travel back and forth, and fortunately was with her when she passed away. So I took some solace in knowing she did not die alone.

My husband and I have been fortunate to have each other and to have travelled extensively around the world. We have met educators from dozens of countries, often through conferences associated with ICET (International Council of Education for Teaching). Our travel has taken us around the globe, from Asia to Africa to Australia, discovering the most delightful and inspiring places.

Irandukht Vahidi Fahmy

For many years, since his arrival in New York, Mahmoud has been involved in intercultural and interfaith understanding, including opening dialogues between Arabs and Jews. I am extremely proud of the peacemaking skills he has brought to this difficult issue.

Following the signing of the Camp David Accords in 1979, Mahmoud and Dr. Abraham Barras, the chief rabbi of Temple Israel in Wilkes Barre, co-chaired a group of dignitaries from our community who embarked on a peace mission to the Middle East in the summer of 1980. The delegation was mostly composed of members of the Jewish community, along with a Presbyterian minister. We spent one week in Egypt and one week in Israel, a groundbreaking travel agenda.

In Egypt, our delegation was welcomed by the most senior government officials, including the Prime Minister. Since Mahmoud's brother Sayed had served as the Interior Minister of Egypt, he assisted our delegation with the agenda. We toured Egypt's major historical sites, including the Pyramids, the Valley of the Kings, and the Aswan Dam. In Israel, we met the foreign minister, Abba Eban, who spoke Arabic fluently. He greeted Mahmoud and said, "I met your brother Sayed." We traveled to Jerusalem, where many prayed in front of Western Wall (or Wailing Wall). Our agenda included visits to Masada, and Eilat, and Nazareth, and Bethlehem in Palestine. For me the most moving moment was visiting the Baha'i World Center in Haifa, with its world famous garden and Universal House of Justice. This was my first and only visit to the center, and I was so moved by its size, beauty, and spirituality. Our two-week trip was an experience that Mahmoud and I would always cherish.

A Checkerboard of Nights and Days

In recent years we've traveled to Qatar, Kuwait, Bahrain, Egypt, and Jordan. In September 1984, my husband took a nine-month sabbatical from his position at Wilkes College and was invited to train the incoming faculty for a brand new university in Qatar. I joined him for three months in Qatar, which is a very small Persian Gulf nation ruled by the Al-Thani family. Most women cover their hair with the hijab (a headscarf), wear an abaya, and socialize separately from men. During our stay, Mahmoud and I lived in the Gulf Hotel, as guests of the government. We found it very luxurious, but ultimately somewhat monotonous.

During our stay I befriended an Iranian couple. The husband, Dr. Ali, was the physician to the royal family. His wife invited me to her friend's house for an elegant women-only tea party. The women guests removed their abayas, under which they were wearing the most fashionable Western designer clothes. I sat next to a beautiful young lady who spoke English and French and was dressed in the latest Paris fashions. She was originally from Lebanon, and invited Mahmoud and me to a dinner at her house with our mutual Iranian friends, Dr. Ali and his wife. Upon the conclusion of the tea party, the women put their abayas back on as their drivers pulled up to meet them.

We accepted the young lady's kind invitation to the dinner, and rode to her home with our friends, Dr. Ali and his wife. When we pulled up, I was astounded. The home was a huge, luxurious mansion, the likes of which I had never seen, even in America. The young lady's much older husband happened to be one of the members of Qatar's ruling family. Although alcohol was forbidden by Muslim law in Qatar, they had a fully-stocked bar. The husband graciously greeted us, but I could not help but notice he had a large glass of whiskey in one hand and prayer beads in the other. His lovely young wife told me that she was his fourth wife, and the other three wives each had their own mansion.

I feel fortunate to be an American citizen who can journey freely around the globe, protected by all the right and privileges that come with being a citizen of this great nation. Our travels have included Hong Kong, China, Taiwan, India, Britain, France, Germany, Denmark, Sweden, Scotland, Norway, Brazil, Argentina, Chile, Mexico, the Bahamas, and Australia.

In Jordan, Mahmoud and I were invited to King Hussein's palace, where we were hosted by Prince Hassan, the king's brother, and his Pakistani wife. In Brunei we were invited by the queen to the palace, where we saw the Arabian horses of the Sultan of Oman. They had built a huge amusement park, like Disney World, next to the palace for their children. In Thailand, we were visited by Mahmoud's niece and her husband, who was serving as Egypt's consul general there. While visiting Japan, we were entertained by my nephew Vafa's in-laws, his wife Yuri's parents.

Mahmoud and I have also travelled all over the U.S., visiting almost every state. One summer, for six weeks, we packed the children into our station wagon and travelled from Pennsylvania to Florida, stopping in every town and city along the way. The children loved seeing the diversity of each city and town, and we had picnics every day, eating the fresh local produce from roadside stands. We took a different route home and did the same thing. I have a great appreciation for the beauty and diversity of my adopted country.

A Checkerboard of Nights and Days

As Mahmoud and I have traveled to dozens of countries and visited countless places, I became a student of culture. I listened to many stories and observed the best and worst in people. We met misguided and power-hungry individuals, as well as knowledgeable, informed, and kind-hearted people. I wondered what shaped people's minds, personalities, and characters. As we listened to their stories, we realized everyone strives for dignity, to be respected and to be loved. Our travels only confirmed a profound lesson: that we must accept and treat everyone as we would like to be treated.

Twenty-One

Thanksgiving is my favorite American holiday. When our family gathers together every year, I often think back to my first Thanksgiving in the United States in November 1957, when I was in Ann Arbor at the University of Michigan. The students, who were from all over the globe—Afghanistan, Pakistan, Iran, Syria, Lebanon, Jordan, Argentina, and Chile—were talking about Thanksgiving break, which I had never heard of before. Our university advisors arranged for local Michigan families to host us on the holiday, and in preparation for this, our house mother invited us to tea to teach us American table etiquette.

When I told the story once, Roya asked me: "Mom, did they assume immigrants didn't know proper manners?"

"No, they simply knew European and Middle Eastern etiquette was quite different from American etiquette. For example, in Iran we often eat our rice and koresh (stew) dinners with a large spoon. In Europe, the tea and place settings are positioned on the table differently."

"Mom, I think you're being too nice."

A Checkerboard of Nights and Days

I spent Thanksgiving in 1957 with a couple in their sixties living on a farm near Ypsilanti, Michigan, a town about twenty minutes from Ann Arbor. The husband was a botanist and sociologist, and the wife belonged to the Baha'i faith and was interested in meeting an Iranian Baha'i. We had a vegetarian Thanksgiving that included delicious organic vegetables and fruits from their farm, and something that tasted like turkey! This couple taught me a lesson on the great American tradition of Thanksgiving that dates back to the Pilgrim days. I loved learning from them and was grateful for their hospitality.

For my second Thanksgiving in November 1958, I was a student at Columbia University and living in Mrs. Goldstein's apartment on Amsterdam Ave. near 125th Street. She was away for Thanksgiving with her son, a famous violinist, so the international student advisor matched me and my Iranian friend Fatima, a New York University political science major, with an African-American family in Harlem, not far from where I lived. We took the bus together there, it was about a ten minute ride. There were twelve family members who greeted us when we arrived. The parents were in their sixties and their son was a New York City policeman. The rest of the family were cousins, aunts, and uncles. Fatima and I arrived in the early afternoon, starving, but we were only served drinks until dinner was served at 5 p.m.

We were served a delicious traditional Thanksgiving turkey dinner, along with something called grits, which we loved, collard greens, which reminded me of the Iranian basket of greens, fried potatoes, and various fruit pies.

By Thanksgiving of 1959, I was engaged to Mahmoud. We lived in student housing in Bancroft Hall and celebrated the holiday with students and friends from the U.S., the Soviet Union, Yugoslavia, Germany, and Egypt. We decided to have an international covered-dish Thanksgiving. Everyone helped themselves to Iranian rice, American turkey, German potato salad, Russian piroshkies, and Polish stuffed cabbage, along with store-bought pies for dessert. I remember thinking that those store-bought pies were not as delicious as the ones I had with the family in Harlem.

In November 1960, I was married to Mahmoud and had a one-month old baby, Roya. We spent Thanksgiving with Salah and Nana Al-Arabi and their 2 ½-year-old daughter Dina, whose favorite activity was climbing into Roya's crib to play with her and the spinning mobile. We cooked together, a mishmash of Egyptian, Iranian and American food and we were all thankful to be in America.

Thirty-seven years later, in 1997, our children would descend upon our family home in Dallas, Pennsylvania with their spouses and children, for an American Thanksgiving celebration. Roya arrived first with her Eastern European/Polish Jewish husband, Daniel. Randa then burst into the door with her husband Michael, an Irish/French Catholic. Finally Raef arrived with his wife Bethanne, and their sons Jared and Trevor.

We lived in a four-story, split level, cream-colored house, with a kidney-shaped swimming pool in the yard. The pool held many happy memories for our children.

In our backyard, I planted a flower and herb garden that reminded me of my childhood in Iran. Every Spring, it would burst forth with flowers, sweet basil, mint, cilantro, chives, leeks, dill, tar-ragon, chives, rosemary, and sage. Nearby was a vegetable garden, which produced everything from lettuce to zucchini to eggplant, a favorite of Mahmoud's.

Our home was decorated with family photos and collectibles from Russia, China, Brazil, Egypt, Iran, Cuba, Czechoslovakia, Holland, India, and South Africa. Carpets from Turkey and paint-ings from Iran and India adorned our walls. In the living room were glass parrots from Brazil, a wooden chair made in Namibia, and one wall was covered with Egyptian papyrus that told the story of the journey to the underworld.

In the kitchen a turkey sizzled in the oven, mashed potatoes sat ready on the counter, gravy simmered on the stove, and a deep dish pumpkin pie rested atop the refrigerator. Our family gath-ered around the dining room table, set with British china and with a decorative silver vase from Egypt as its centerpiece.

I reflected back on our family, on all the various paths my chil-dren had taken to bring us to this day. Roya had moved to Los Angeles, met and married Daniel, a rabbi, and integrated into the Jewish faith. When Daniel spoke at an honorary dinner for Mahmoud, he remarked, "I'm the only rabbi with a Muslim father in-law named Mahmoud!"

Randa moved to Washington D.C., married a Catholic man named Michael, and integrated that faith into their family. Raef married Bethanne, a young lady with Jewish and Catholic roots whose maternal grandmother escaped the Holocaust by travelling through China and landing in Philadelphia.

Through the years we had celebrated each other's successes and joys, and supported each other through dark times and tragedies. As we gathered around the Thanksgiving table, we offered Muslim, Baha'i, Jewish, and Christian prayers. Through the years we had celebrated christenings, Bat Mitzvahs, confirmations, Rosh Hashanah, Yom Kippur, Nowruz, Eid Al-Fitr, and the festival of Ridvan.

I reflected back on how we hadn't brought up our children in any religion. We decided that they would choose for themselves someday. One girlfriend broke up with Raef over this issue. She came from a different faith and her parents asked him what religion he practiced.

"My mother is Baha'i and my father is a Muslim."

"What are you?" she asked.

"I don't believe in any religion," Raef answered firmly.

He chose his own path, as all my children did, and I am proud that they have done so. That is a freedom that I never would have denied them. When Roya told me she was engaged to a Jewish man, I asked her whether he was a good man and if she loved him. When she answered "yes" to both, that was all Mahmoud and I needed to hear.

As I looked around the table at my family, I reflected on how much I had changed over the years. I realized that I inherited my mother's personality. I'm a perfectionist who can be very critical—my husband likes to call me "The General." But my husband changed me. If I had married someone other than Mahmoud, I probably would not have stayed married because I am not an easy person to live with.

I learned so much from him. I learned not to be so critical, not so judgmental. Roya once said to me, "Mom, you criticized me so much. You always told me to do this, to do that." That was a problem. I admitted it and I changed.

Early on I wondered if my marriage to Mahmoud would work because he was a more optimistic and easy going person than me. But his kindness and patience mellowed me over the years and helped to smooth my rougher edges. He would always tell me, "Iran, please sit down. Please relax. Take it easy." I finally took his advice and I learned from him. Our differences worked in harmony and made us both better people.

Raef's two young sons, Jared and Trevor, were with us on that Thanksgiving. In the next four years three more girls would join us: Randa's daughter Alexandria, who she named after Mahmoud's birthplace, Raef's daughter Kira, and Alana, Roya's adopted daughter from India, born Hindu but converted into the Jewish faith.

Mahmoud sat at the head of the table with his back to the sun porch. I sat at the other end of the table, with my back to the living room with its paintings, statues, and artifacts from all seven continents. Glancing into our yard, I saw a dusting of snow glittering on the grass. It reminded me of a poem Roya wrote for Raef when she was 10. He had a morning newspaper route and came home one day

Irandukht Vahidi Fahmy

with snow all over his face. Roya said to him, "You have icicles on your eyelashes" and wrote a poem with those lines.

Our table was laden with a classic Thanksgiving spread—roasted turkey, cornbread stuffing, pumpkin pie, cranberry compote with oranges, and mashed potatoes. But there were also grape leaves stuffed with fresh ground lamb and rice, hummus drizzled with olive oil and lemon juice, and fresh pita bread that I got up early in the morning to bake.

Later we would drink Turkish coffee boiled in a metal container called a kanaka and served in tiny cups. The tea would be served in delicate Persian glasses. And there was soda for the adults and milk and juices for the children.

Our family tradition includes prayers before the meal—prayers from the Baha'i, Jewish, Christian, and Muslim traditions, spoken in Farsi, Arabic, Hebrew, and English.

Mahmoud always starts with the Arabic prayer, "Bism'allah al Rahman a'Rahim" ("In the name of Allah, the Merciful One..."). He names the attributes of God—all powerful, all compassionate, all knowing, and all seeing.

Roya's husband Daniel continues in Hebrew: "Baruch atah Adonai, Eloheinu melech haolam, hamotzi lechem min ha-aretz" ("Blessed are you our God, ruler of the universe, who brings forth bread from the earth").

I quietly demurred when asked to give a Baha'i prayer, but Roya, the spiritually curious one in the family, encouraged me.

off

180

A Checkerboard of Nights and Days

"Mom, please! The prayers are so uplifting. Just say something—anything!"

So I opened a small book of Baha'i writings and read:

> *The purpose of*
> *religion...is to*
> *establish unity and*
> *concord amongst*
> *the peoples of the*
> *world: make it*
> *not the cause*
> *of dissension*
> *and strife.*

Roya asked me, "Mom, what drew you to choose the Baha'i faith?"

I told the story once again, how my maternal grandmother and grandfather were born Muslim, but my parents and grandparents became followers of Bahá'u'lláh, converted by my paternal grandfather, a teacher and pioneer in the faith and one of the "first believers."

Mahmoud chimed in: "My mother and father were born in Alexandria, Egypt, and were very spiritual and pious Muslims, but not fanatics or extremists. Our family, friends, and neighbors were Armenians, Jews, and Copts. In fact, my first watch was given to me as a gift by my Jewish friend." He noted that this year, Thanksgiving, Hanukkah, and Ramadan were all being celebrated around the same time, and all three revolve around friends, family, food, and prayer."

"Throughout the world they are celebrating Ramadan and giving to the poor. For some families the tradition is to celebrate the end of Ramadan's 30 days of fasting with the holiday of Eid Al-Fitr. A lamb is slaughtered at a butcher shop according to Halal law, which is very similar to Kosher law. When I was young, our family would walk around Alexandria and give sections of the lamb to poor families so they would have dinner on Eid Al-Fitr.

"In the 1980s," Mahmoud continued, "when Iran and I were in Cairo, an old man in his late seventies knocked at the door of my brother's house. We were expecting his visit, and my brother gave him his packaged lamb, enough for his children and grandchildren. There is the belief that the poor possess a sacred spirit and that we must feed them. This man had been coming to their house for years for his food. He bowed, prayed, and left. The whole neighborhood was full of tents with free food for poor people so they could eat and celebrate—huge dishes of rice, beans, lentils, bread, and meat."

"Dad," Raef said, "I couldn't fast for thirty days."

Roya added: "I couldn't last without morning coffee and daily chocolate."

"My latest diet feels like I am always fasting!" said Randa

Mahmoud smiled. "As soon as the sun rises, no food, no water, nothing touches your lips. It's a way of honoring God." He nodded to Daniel, who returned it, knowing how hard fasting is during Yom Kippur.

A Checkerboard of Nights and Days

My children now started reminiscing about the dinner parties Mahmoud and I would host when they were young—the grape leaves, tabbouleh, hummus, shish kabob, rice, and baklava desserts that were especially prepared for the guests. They also shared memories of sneaking chocolate-covered cherries that were displayed in our crystal candy dishes for the guests.

Twenty-Two

It's the evening of my birthday, December 21st, the winter solstice. I've built a fire in the fireplace and I'm watching the weather report on television. I look outside through the large glass sliding door in my family room and notice the thick white snow covering the ground. The snow on the trees looks like white flower buds. Heaps of snow form small hills on the in-ground swimming pool. I hear the sound of the wind, like a piano being tuned. I am mesmerized—suddenly the snowflakes looked like synchronized dancers whirling through the air.

The phone rings, bringing me out of my immersion in nature.

"Happy Birthday, my sister!" It is Manoochehr calling from San Diego. "Do you remember that it is Shab e Yelda?"

Of course I remember. I was born on that ancient Zoroastrian holiday that marks the beginning of winter, a celebration of its darkest nights and short days.

Manoochehr tells me he's having a big party. His three children—Virasb, Mahsa, and Pantea—are with him, along with his wife Delara and five grandchildren. As we talk, he tells me that Pooran has just walked in with her son Vafa, daughter-in-law Yuri, and her grandson Kian. "The cousins and their families are also here," Manoochehr says, "along with my uncle's son Farhad and his Columbian wife Malena."

I ask a very Iranian question: "What are you serving?"

"Delara has spread a beautiful sofreh full of Persian food. Do you remember in Iran how we would save watermelon from the summer in the cool basement and serve it on winter nights? That's what we're having, along with dried fruits, sunflower seeds, pumpkin seeds, pistachio nuts, and the famous Noghl candies from Rezaiyeh."

Noghl, or sugar-coated almonds with rose water, are made only in the city of my childhood.

"Cousin Cyrus brought it special for us from Rezaiyeh," Manoochehr says, "along with Ghaz." Ghaz is a Persian candy made with sugar or corn syrup, egg whites, almonds, pistachios, and rosewater.

"Mahsa brought the American chocolate, of course!" my brother continues. "I hope next year you will be with us to celebrate your birthday and Shab e Yelda."

I smile. "Do you have fire in your fireplace?" Having one is a tradition on this holiday.

"Of course!" says Manoochehr.

Another tradition of Shab e Yelda is to gather with families and friends and read the poetry of Hafiz, Omar Khayyám, and Saadi Shirazi. These lines from Shirazi, which I have always remembered, are written for the darkest night of year.

Like all my pain, there is still the hope of recovery,
like the eve of Yelda, there will finally be an end.
After winter night of Shab e Yelda, a transformation
takes place, the waiting is over, light shines and goodness prevails.
The sight of each morning is New Year. And the night
of departure is the eve of Yelda.

The loss of Pooran, my only sister, in July 2015 was a tremendous blow for me. She passed away in San Diego at the age of 85. We had been very close throughout childhood. She was a wonderful sister, a remarkable and selfless person. She took care of family, relatives, and friends, always putting the needs of others before her own. She had amazing powers of persuasion and determination, and was kind, caring, and helpful to all. I miss her advice and support, and dream of her often.

In Iran she taught high school English and later became dean of the College of Translation in Tehran. She came to the U.S. in 1980, after the Islamic revolution; her only son Vafa was already attending college in San Diego. She loved the U.S. and lived a simple life in the Del Mar neighborhood of San Diego. She assisted Iranian refugees with resettlement in American and helped them to adapt to the culture.

She had worked very hard since she was a young girl, helping to support my mother after my father died. I knew that she was often hurt by the cutting remarks of my mother, but Pooran never responded in kind; she kept her pain inside.

In the U.S. she would help immigrants with translation, take them to the immigration office, and help them with driver's license applications. In her later years, she went every day to the local senior citizens' center, where there were a lot of immigrants from different countries, and helped them with translation.

Her son Vafa married a wonderful woman from Japan named Yuriko (Yuri) whom he had met while in college in San Diego. Pooran was like a mother to Yuri because her own mother was in Japan.

Her generosity always amazed me. If someone gave her a gift, she would give it to a needy person. She gave away her jewelry to me and to her daughter-in-law. When she died Pooran had $200 in her savings account. She had given everything away to help others.

In my dreams Pooran and I are together in Iran, going to visit friends. We share our deepest thoughts and feelings. One night I dreamed I was with her in our childhood home in Rezaiyeh. She was walking away from me and I kept asking her, "Poori Joon, my sister, where are you going?" Our mother wasn't there; it was only the two of us, standing in our living room, and through the windows I could see our beautiful garden, the profusion of flowers and fruit trees. Then I woke up.

As I grew older, I not only appreciated more and more how Pooran helped hold the family together after my father's death, but also how hard it had been for my mother to be left alone with four young children and no income. It was right after World War II, a terrible time when everyone had struggles and couldn't help each other. But Pooran was always there whenever we needed her. She enjoyed life by giving to others.

Twenty-Three

Roya once asked me, "Was there a moment where you finally felt you were an American?

There was no specific time; rather, it was a feeling of identity and belonging that developed over time. Like my children, I had the advantage of knowing American culture better than most Americans themselves, because I had another culture with which to compare it. I have been all over the world and I know that the U.S. is the best country in the world to live in. There is no question about it. I love this country and I feel very American.

Yet to this day some people still don't see me as American. Partly it's my looks and partly it's my accent.

The point when I felt more comfortable with the language and being truly American was when I began working at the Children's Service Center, the best learning experience I ever had. The friendships I made and the experience of working with developmentally challenged children changed my life.

But it's very hard for me to say what being an American really means. I never gave up many aspects of my Iranian culture.

Mahmoud and I took what was best in Iranian and Egyptian culture and what was best in American culture to raise our children.

In Iran, decisions were made for me, not by me; in the United States, I had the freedom to make my own decisions. That was very important for me. I'm a naturally independent person but in Iran I couldn't be independent. As a child, I always was told what to do and what not to do. I never liked anyone ordering me to make decisions against my will.

How you were raised deeply affects you and you can't escape it. I grew up in a world of social and cultural restriction, a protected life where I had to follow the cultural code of my family and my people whether I agreed with it or not. All that was changed by coming to the United States of America where I could finally be my true self.

Was it fate that I was awarded a Royal Scholarship, one of only twenty students in a nation of millions? Why had it happened to me? Looking back now, it was a combination of luck, timing, and hard work.

It is a late spring day in 2015, and Mahmoud and I finally decide to downsize our home. We pack up and move out of our large family home in Dallas, where we raised our three children. We bid farewell to our wonderful house, gardens and the kidney shaped pool, the site of many happy memories. We move to a smaller one story villa near the local golf-course and country club. As usual, I wake up early, brew the coffee, and walk into the new sunroom, open the door, and enter a small patio. A pleasant, cool breeze welcomes me. I take a deep breath, filling my lungs with fresh air.

A Checkerboard of Nights and Days

The sun already peeks through the clouds and birds are starting to awaken. The aroma of sweet basil, cilantro, and tarragon in my small garden fills the air. The impatiens are in full bloom, and the view of my neighbor's well-kept miniature garden, crammed with a mix of beautiful flowers, is breathtaking. The beauty of nature puts me in a trance, almost a dream world, as an extraordinary calmness sweeps over me.

I now feel such a warm tranquility and clarity of mind. I find myself contemplating the years, months, and days that have gone by as I approach the golden years of my life. My father, my mother, my sister, and my best friends are in heaven. I think back on my life, on all the twists and turns that it has taken, grateful that I ended up in the best country in the world. There is no such thing as absolute happiness, but I am very content.

I hear the magical voice of my beloved father reciting poetry from *The Rubaiyat of Omar Khayyám*:

> *Oh, come with old Khayyám, and leave the Wise*
> *To talk one thing is certain, that Life flies;*
> *One thing is certain, and the Rest is Lies;*
> *The flower that once has blown forever dies.*

My memories of Iran now consist of nature, of the trees along the canal where I lived, of the aqua blue colors of Lake Rezaiyeh and the forlorn salt pillars that towered along its shores, of the treasures of the abundant garden in the courtyard of my childhood home. I remember it exactly, for it is forever embedded in my mind—the garden filled with roses, pansies, begonias, gladiolas, anemones, irises, and jasmines. The oasis of fruit trees—plum,

191

pear, peach, apple, apricot, persimmon, and flowering almond, along with climbing grapevines. The pool of spring water in the center of the courtyard, where I would wash my face in the morning, so clear and pure that I could see the pebbles at the very bottom. And the magnificent cherry tree that towered so high above us.

Yes, time flies, as the wise philosopher Khayyám has said. Everything is impermanent, all beings will die, nothing will live forever. I have lived a long and complicated life, and have taken many journeys. I have walked into uncharted territories, immersing myself in cultures and languages entirely foreign to me. My journey has been full of bumps and twists and turns. I have experienced isolation, loneliness, racism, religious intolerance, and the death of my father at a young age. I have also experienced great kindness, caring, triumph, and joy. I always had people who guided me, aided me, and taught me about new ways of life.

I never gave up hope or abandoned my aspirations. I came to know my strengths and weaknesses. I always searched for truth, expanded my knowledge, explored innovative ideas, and tried to understand what it meant to be part of a community. My salvation in life has been my flexibility, my resilience, and my lifelong search for knowledge: self-knowledge and knowledge of the world through which I have passed.

When I came to the United States, I fell in love with this country. It is my one and only home. I have travelled all over the world, and yet I still cherish the original American ideals of social justice, personal responsibility and peace above those of any other country.

A Checkerboard of Nights and Days

These ideals are epitomized through a poem displayed in the United Nations building in New York City by the great Persian poet Saadi:

The sons of Adam are limbs of each other,
Having been created of one essence.
When the calamity of time affects one limb
The other limbs cannot remain at rest.
If you have no sympathy for the troubles of others,
You are unworthy to be called by the name of a Human.

I believe with all my heart that every person has the same desire to live in peace, unity and freedom. Through my journey, I have come to believe our destiny is not predetermined for us, but is always ours to create anew as we live our lives day by day in consideration for others.

Today I dream more often about the past, and sometimes I remember these dreams when I awaken. I dream about my mother, who is asking me, "Where have you gone? You have left me and I am lonely." I dream about my sister, who tells me, "I feel free in America."

Not long ago I had an extremely vivid dream where I heard my father's voice. He was reciting a poem from Omar Khayyám. I woke up suddenly and remembered Manoochehr reciting the same poem when I visited him in California recently:

Tis all a Chequer-board of Nights and Days
Where Destiny with Men for Pieces plays
Hither and thither moves, and mates, and slays,
And one by one back in the Closet lays.

Irandukht Vahidi Fahmy

My life has been such a checkerboard, with so many tides and forces that have affected me, so many dark black nights and brilliant white days. I will always cherish that past, just as I have always embraced the present with open arms. It has been my great fortune to live in the United States of America, a country whose culture encourages personal responsibility, where everyone has rights and dignity, and where I could finally find the freedom to be myself, a freedom I had been searching for my entire life.

Made in the USA
Columbia, SC
11 September 2018